The Rich Heritage of Stewart Memorial United Methodist Church

Figure 1: Stewart Methodist Episcopal Church
Rev. W.P. Pickins, Pastor

The Rich Heritage of Stewart Memorial United Methodist Church

Jake C. Miller, Ph.D.

with a foreword by
Walter E. Monroe, Jr. D.D., D.H.L.

Backintyme
Palm Coast, Florida U.S.A.

Correspondence and orders may be addressed to:
Stewart Memorial United Methodist Church
317 N. Martin Luther King Blvd.
Daytona Beach FL 32114
Telephone: 386-255-7222
Website: www.ourchurch.com/member/s/stewartmemumc

Cover design by Joel V. Fears, Sr.

Published by Backintyme,
A subsidiary of Boxes and Arrows, Inc.

Backintyme Publishing
30 Medford Drive
Palm Coast FL 32137-2504

Telephone: 860-468-9631
Email: sales@backintyme.com
Website: http://backintyme.com/publishing.php

ISBN: 978-0939479-351
Printed in the United States of America
Library of Congress Control Number: 2011911830

Dedication

To persons who, through their services to Stewart Memorial, have made and are continuing to make valuable contributions to the Christian cause. Among those persons some are deceased, some are serving in churches elsewhere, and some are still with us. Whether their services were short-lived or for a lifetime, their efforts are appreciated. and to them this book is dedicated.

Contents

List of Figures

Foreword

By Walter E. Monroe, Jr., Senior Pastor,
Stewart Memorial United Methodist Church

Have you ever wondered about the people God chose to start Stewart Memorial? Did they make mistakes? Were they ever disagreeable? How did they deal with disappointments? How did they come up with the necessary finances to erect this building? What is the connection between this congregation and the United Methodist Church? What did they have that you have not?

There are some real answers to those questions in the pages of this book. Many of the chapters are short stories about individuals, events and experiences that transpired over several decades. But all the stories taken as a whole tell a much greater tale than any single one. Instead of a people with exceptional abilities and character, it tells of a people who were prone to disappointment. Instead of a struggle between lifestyles and cultural heritage, it shows a struggle between the temporal and divine.

We have come a long way since our humble beginnings. Stewart Memorial was founded 1893 under the leadership of the Rev. Thomas H. B. Walker. The church was originally located in a little white house on the corner of Second Avenue (now Dr. Mary McLeod Bethune Boulevard) and Spruce Street in Daytona Beach. It was in 1972 when the church relocated to its present structure, 317 North Dr. Martin L. King, Jr. Boulevard.

There is no question in my mind that the church was and is a place where people can go and be themselves and really "bear each other's burdens"[1] and share each other's pains, cares, and joys. The church is also a place that offers people an opportunity to live as faithful servants of God and as faithful servants to humanity.

Sincere gratitude is hereby expressed to Dr. Jake Miller, a former political science professor at Bethune-Cookman University and an active lay member of this congregation. It is due to his diligence and research that we now have a document that amply depicts the history of the church. He has made us keenly aware of the vision, mission, contributions, successes and challenges of the church locally, nationally and worldwide. Because this book is an up-to-date history of the significant role in the life of the church, it can help people like you and me have a deeper appreciation of the work of Christ in this congregation.

Because this book shows the richness of our heritage as an affirmation of Christ's unifying and liberating power in the world, it should be a required resource for every church leader and member. It should also be a useful resource for congregations and churches at large to point to the hope of tomorrow.

---

[1] Galatians 6:2.

Preface

In 2006, the writer accepted the task of writing the history of Stewart Memorial United Methodist Church. Realizing that there are no persons available who were present when the church was founded in 1893 and that recorded information is limited, the writer, with great trepidation accepted the task, knowing that the document that would emerge would represent the history as reflected by the documents and human resources that were available.

This document relied strongly on earlier historic sketches beginning with the "Historical Data," supplied by H. C. McLain and Dr. T. A. Adams for use in the Forty-Fourth Anniversary Souvenir Program of 1937. Both of the authors were identified with Stewart Memorial when it was in its infancy. McLain was a member as early as 1904, and could possibly have been earlier. Adams was a member by 1911, if not earlier. Valuable also were the "Historical Statement," which appeared in the souvenir booklet of the Service of Consecration and Open House of April 15, 1973, and the "Historical Reflection" submitted by Sarah B. Burns for use in the souvenir program of the Centennial Celebration in 1993. Burns was a longtime member, whose membership goes back to the time of the McLain-Adams writing. Later updates of the history appeared at the time of the 105th anniversary by Shirley Moore and Shirley Bing, and in the program of the 110th anniversary by Joel Fears, Sr. All of the historical statements, cited above, were helpful in the preparation of this document, and sincere thanks are expressed to the writers.

Also important in writing this document were the old minutes available from Joel Fears, the archivist, and Jessie Childs and Vera Barragan, both of whom served as administrative assistants. Nell Thrift, of the Florida Conference UMC Archive was helpful. Valuable information also was provided by Walter Monroe (pastor), Willie Scott, Gladys Greene, Agnes Fair and Marian Rivers. Thanks must also be given to others who provided information or gave interviews. Their contributions are noted in the document. Among the readers of the manuscript were Jessie Childs, Sallie Shelton Culver, Joel Fears, Sr., Mary Fears, Collace Greene, and Gladys Greene. Without their reading, this book would have been impossible. Thanks to them for a job well done.

The many photographs in this book were provided by Joel Fears, and to him we owe a debt of gratitude. Pictures best describe the historical account of Stewart Memorial.

As the denomination grew and progressed, so did Stewart Memorial; thus, as a prelude to viewing the historic development of the church, we begin by looking at its roots in Methodism.

Chapter 1

Stewart Memorial's Roots in Methodism

Founded in 1893, Stewart Memorial United Methodist Church has its roots deep in Methodism. As the denomination grew and progressed, so did the local church. Methodism was inspired by John Wesley, an ordained priest of the Church of England, and his brother, Charles, who is better known as a hymnist. John was born in Epsworth, England in 1703 and his brother was born four years later. In 1725, the brothers entered Oxford and founded the *Holy Club* or *Methodists*, as they were called. Both brothers came to the colony of Georgia (in the present United States) as missionaries of the Anglican Church (Church of England) in March 1736, but disillusioned with their lack of progress, they returned—Charles in December 1736 and John in 1738.[1]

Upon their return to England, the brothers had their Aldersgate experience, which transformed their beliefs. In the Journal of John Wesley, May 24, 1738 this description of that experience is offered:

In the evening I went very unwillingly to a society

---

[1] *The Book of Discipline of the United Methodist Church*, 1996, 9-10.

in Aldersgate Street, where one was reading
Luther's preface to the Epistle to the Romans.
About a quarter before nine, while the leader
was describing the change which God works in
the heart through faith in Christ, I felt my heart
strangely warmed. I felt I did trust in Christ alone
for salvation; and an assurance was given me that
He had taken away my sins, even mine, and saved
me from the law of sin and death.[2]

According to the *Book of Discipline*, because of this experience, the Wesley brothers "succeeded in leading a lively renewal
movement in the Church of England." As the Methodist Movement grew, some of those involved made trips to the New World
and settled in Maryland, Virginia, New York and Pennsylvania.
John Wesley, the head of the Methodist Movement, sent several
lay preachers to America in 1769, including Francis Asbury,
who was regarded the most influential.[3]

One of the major events in the development of Methodism in the colonies was the Conference of Methodist Preachers
that convened in Philadelphia in 1773. In addition to pledging
their loyalty to the leadership of John Wesley, the ten preachers agreed to refrain from administering the sacraments because
they were laypersons. They decided that the sacraments of Baptism and the Lord's Supper would be administered by local Anglican ministers. They also agreed to hold regular conferences
to conduct the business of the Methodist Movement.[4]

Following the independence of the colonies, Wesley sent
Thomas Coke to the United States to assist Asbury with the
leadership of the Movement. Coke brought with him a pamphlet
entitled "Sunday Services of the Methodists in North America,"
which incorporated Wesley's revision of the 39 articles of the

---

[2]Wesley's Aldersgate experience:
<http//www/gbgm-umc.org/aldersgate-wheaton/aumcname.html>.
  [3]*The Book of Discipline of the United Methodist Church*, 1996, 10.
  [4]Idem.

Church of England.[5]

In 1784, at the Christmas Conference of Preachers, the Methodist Episcopal Church in America was organized, and Asbury and Cokes were named the first two bishops. Attending this conference were two African Americans—Richard Allen and Harry Hosier. Following this, the church published its first Discipline, and in 1792 the church held its first Quadrennial General Conference. In 1808 the Methodist Episcopal Church drafted its first Constitution.[6]

Shortly after the church was established, it began to fall apart. Issues of "race" relations, slavery and general church policies caused a split, and the formation of other churches. Richard Allen, an emancipated slave, left the church because of "racial" mistreatment, and in 1816 formed the African Methodist Episcopal (AME) Church. Another group left because of "racial" problems and in 1821 organized the African Methodist Episcopal Zion Church. The issue of slavery brought about additional splits, including the one that resulted in the creation of the Methodist Episcopal Church South in 1845. In 1870, the memberships of African Americans in the South were transferred to the Colored Methodist Episcopal Church, now known as Christian Methodist Episcopal (CME) Church.[7]

In 1868, with the nation in general disarray following the American Civil War, the Methodist Episcopal Church began to form mission churches for freed Blacks in the south. It was out of these mission efforts that Stewart Memorial Methodist Episcopal Church was founded in 1893. In 1939, when several Methodist Churches reunited and assumed the title *Methodist Church*, Black Methodist Episcopal Churches were included, but they were placed in the segregated Central Jurisdiction of the Methodist Church.[8] Stewart Memorial Episcopal Church was renamed *Stewart Memorial Methodist Church*. There was

---

[5]Ibid., 11.

[6]Idem.

[7]Ibid., 13-15.

[8]Ibid., 17.

still another change to come. When several Methodist-based churches united in 1967 and became the United Methodist Church,[9] Stewart Memorial assumed its present name, *Stewart Memorial United Methodist Church.*

Through the years, the United Methodist Church evolved, and so did Stewart Memorial, but the basis foundation of Methodism was unshakeable. Methodism, as perceived by John Wesley, emphasized small group worship, which was described as:

> A company of men having the form and seeking the power of godliness, united in order to pray together, to receive the word of exhortation, and to watch over one another in love, that they may help each other to work out their salvation.[10]

Making up these small groups under Wesley were those who had "a desire to flee from the wrath to come, and to be saved from their sins."[11] Historically, Methodists were expected to demonstrate their faith by

> doing no harm, by avoiding evil of every kind, especially that which is most generally practiced ...doing good of every kind merciful after their power; as they have opportunity, doing good of every possible sort, and, as far as possible, to all men...By attending upon all the ordinances of God; such are: the public worship of God...."[12]

It is upon the sound foundation of Methodism, as emphasized by Wesley, that Stewart Memorial was founded and continues to exist.

---

[9]Ibid., 19.
[10]Ibid., 62, 70.
[11]Ibid., 62.2, 70-71
[12]Ibid., 52.2, 70.

Chapter 2

Stewart Memorial and Methodism in Florida

Presently, Stewart Memorial is a part of the Florida Conference of the United Methodist Church, but that was not always the case. "Racial" segregation was a crucial factor in the development of the church, just as it was in the general society. On January 29, 1873, Euro-Americans from the North and a few African Americans from South Carolina, who were concerned with meeting the needs of freed slaves in Florida, met in Jacksonville, Florida and organized an Annual Conference. They were supported by the Freedmen's Aid Society, a part of the church that supplied food, clothing, medicine and protection for the needy, regardless of "race." In 1883, because of strained relations, White members requested that the General Conference allow them to form a separate conference. In 1886 the Florida Conference approved the separation. Thus, with the departure of the Whites, the Florida Conference, with the exception of one member, became a Black conference.[1] As a struggling conference, it sought to strengthen itself by looking Southward, and among the new churches it organized was Stewart Memo-

---

[1] John A. Simpson, "Historical Sketches of the Florida Annual Conference (CJ) of Methodist Church" (manuscript), June 24, 1965, 1.

rial Methodist Episcopal Church which, through the efforts of Thomas H. B. Walker, was founded in 1893.[2]

In 1912, because of the size of the state and travel difficulties, the General Conference was asked to allow the Southern part of the state to be formed into the South Florida Mission. The Florida Conference perfected the change in 1913, and Jeffery Grant was appointed its first superintendent. Others who followed him as superintendent were: P. A. Daniels, S. A. Huger (1917) and W. H. Bartley (1918).[3]

A milestone was reached in 1921, when the Mission organized itself into the South Florida Mission Conference with two districts—the Atlantic and Gulf. J. A. Simpson became the Superintendent of the Atlantic District in which Stewart Memorial was affiliated. When the Mission Conference met in Bradenton in 1925, the strength it had gained allowed it to organize into an annual conference. Two years later, John Wesley replaced John A. Simpson as superintendent.[4]

After 1925, the South Florida Mission Conference held its annual meeting in Miami and Clearwater before convening in Daytona Beach in 1928. This was the first time that members of Stewart Memorial were able to attend such a gathering in large numbers. W. P. Pickens, the future pastor of Stewart Memorial served as recorder for the Conference.[5]

Again in 1935, the Conference convened in Daytona Beach, with Robert E. Jones, one of the first Black bishops, presiding.[6] Serving as recorder for this meeting was another future pastor, C. R. A. Banks.

In January 1939, the Annual Conference again convened

---

[2]H. C. McLain and Dr. T. A. Adams, "Historical Data," The Celebration of the Forty-Fourth Anniversary of Stewart Memorial Methodist Episcopal Church, December 15-19, 1937, 3.

[3]Simpson (1965), 8.

[4]Idem.

[5]Robert Temple, Jr., *Florida Flame: A History of the Florida Conference of the United Methodist Church* (Nashville: Parthenon Press, 1987), appendixes.

[6]Simpson (1965), 10.

at Stewart Memorial with its bishop, Edgar Blake, presiding. At that conference, Mary McLeod Bethune was elected lay delegate to the General Convention. Shortly after the uniting Conference of 1939, Bishop Shaw called a meeting in Daytona Beach and announced to the delegates that the church was assuming the name "Methodist Church," and that the Conference was being placed in the Central Jurisdiction.[7] Thus, Stewart Memorial Methodist Episcopal Church became Stewart *Memorial Methodist Church.*

Figure 2.1: At Bethune-Cookman College

Annual Conference at Bethune-Cookman College

After being placed in the Central Jurisdiction, the South Florida Conference, presided over by Bishop J. W. E. Bowen, met in Daytona Beach in 1950.[8] In 1952, the South Florida Confer-

---

[7]Ibid., 12.
[8]Simpson (1965), 16.

ence, which was formed because of inadequate means of transportation, merged with the Florida Conference, thus making one conference in Florida for African Americans.[9] Following the merger, the new Florida Conference met in Daytona Beach on a regular basis—1953, 1959, 1962, 1964-1968. Rogers P. Fair, pastor of Stewart Memorial, served as recorder of the South Florida Conference from 1949-1952 and for the Florida Conference from 1957 -1969.[10] The conferences, held in Daytona Beach, afforded members of Stewart Memorial greater opportunity to attend the Annual Conference.

The early ministers of Stewart Memorial were active in the South Florida and the Florida Conferences. Many of them served as secretaries for the Annual Conferences. Scott Bradley served in 1906 and 1907, Thomas Huger 1947 and 1948, W. Pickens from 1922-1930, and C. R. A. Banks from 1932 -1946.[11]

Likewise, several of the ministers were appointed to serve as district superintendents, including:

• Thomas Walker - Gainesville District, 1943.

• Scott Bradley - Jacksonville District, 1931 and Lake City District, 1922.

• Thomas Huger - Gulf District, 1942 and Jacksonville District, 1952.

• S. D. Bankston – Atlantic District, 1937 and Gulf District, 1954.

• C. R. A. Banks - Gulf District, 1946.

• D. S. Selmore - Gulf District, 1925, 1937 and Atlantic District, 1936.

[9]Ibid., 17.
[10]Temple (1987), 383-84.
[11]Ibid., appendix.

- W. Pickens – Gulf District, 1931.[12]

In 1967, the three branches of Methodism united. With this unification, the Methodist Church became the United Methodist Church. With this change, Stewart Memorial Methodist Church became Stewart Memorial United Methodist Church, and almost from the beginning, its members became active with the United Methodist Church, on the district, conference, jurisdictional, general and global levels.

---

[12]Temple (1987), appendix.

Chapter 3

Beginning of a Historic Journey

The settlement of Daytona was founded by Mathias Day in 1870, and was incorporated in 1876, with two African Americans—John Tolliver and Thaddeus Gooden—among the 26 citizens who signed the petition requesting incorporation as a city.[1] During this period of history, African Americans participated in the political community, with few restrictions. Most of them, however, were Republicans, since state laws prohibited their participation in the affairs of the Democratic Party. A few years later, things changed drastically, with segregation imposing unthinkable restrictions on voting.

Following the Civil War, large numbers of African Americans were brought to the Port Orange area by John Milton Hawks, a White abolitionist, and in later years, some of them moved northward to the Daytona community. The construction of the Florida East Coast railroad, also, attracted Blacks to the area. Other African Americans were employed in turpentine camps, lumberyards and the newly developed tourist indus-

---

[1]Leonard Lempel, "Mary McLeod Bethune and Early Daytona's African American Community," *Halifax Herald*, Vol. 16, No. 2 (December 1998), 2-3.

try. Most of the Blacks of Daytona lived in the communities of Midway and Waycross. and later in Newtown.[2] Although Mt. Bethel Baptist Church and Mount Zion A.M.E. Church existed in Daytona before 1893,[3] no church existed in the Midway area at that time. Perhaps, with these thoughts in mind, a nineteen-year-old Methodist evangelist came to Daytona and found fertile ground for founding a Methodist Episcopal Church, which later became Stewart Memorial United Methodist Church.

Figure 3.1: Thomas Hamilton Beb Walker

After conducting several successful evangelistic services in the South Florida Mission, Thomas Hamilton Beb Walker, a native of Tallahassee, came to Daytona Beach in 1893. He organized a mission church. He served the pastoral charge for two years before being transferred to Simpson Methodist Episcopal Church in Jacksonville, Florida.[4] Walker brought to Daytona a religious faith which had existed in the United States for approximately a hundred and twenty years. This new church was a mission of the Methodist Episcopal Church—a denomination that had been victimized by racism. In spite of its division, however, there were many who viewed

---

[2]Idem.

[3]H. C. McLain and Dr. T. A. Adams, "Historical Data," The Celebration of the Forty-Fourth Anniversary of Stewart Memorial Methodist Episcopal Church, December 15-19, 1937, 3.

[4]Thomas Yenser, ed., *Who's Who in Colored America, 1941-to-1944*, 6th ed. (Brooklyn: Thomas Yenser, 1942), 535.

the Methodist Church as one church.[5]

While seeking to establish a church in Daytona, Thomas Walker was compelled to fight against many obstacles, including mosquitoes, hot weather, and other inconveniences. The mosquitoes were overcome somewhat by what was known as mosquito brushes and smudge pots, and dedicated worshippers resisted some of the summer heat with personal hand fans. Unfortunately, the early congregation was not familiar with such conveniences as electricity, running water, and telephone services. Also at this time, transportation was primitive.[6] In spite of these conditions, there were those who had the desire to worship God, and these formed the foundation of the present-day Stewart Memorial.

In order to survive, a new church does not only need members, but a sanctuary as well. An act of generosity by M.L. Stewart, a retired minister who resided in Daytona Beach during the winter months, enabled the church to acquire a small white building and place it on the corner of Second Avenue (Mary McLeod Bethune Blvd.) and Spruce Street. In gratitude for such a gift, the members named the building Stewart Chapel in honor of the donor.[7]

Following the pastorate of Thomas Walker, many well-trained ministers came to Daytona Beach to provide leadership for the newly established church. Among the earlier ones were: S. Middleton, L.J. Littles, O.B. Jackson, Albert Emanuel, B.J. Shannon, O.M. Irving, Scott Bartley, G..B. Wilson, D.S. Elmore, Joseph Deas, and G.B. Lennon.[8]

No records are available to suggest the nature of services or their regularity. Nevertheless, a column written by Albert Emanuel in the *Daytona Gazette News* of April 6, 1901, an-

---

[5]Robert Temple, Jr., *Florida Flame: A History of the Florida Conference of the United Methodist Church* (Nashville: Parthenon Press, 1987).

[6]Ianthe Bond Hebel, *Centennial History of Volusia County 1854 -1954*, Volusia County Historical Commission (Daytona Beach College, 1955) 94.

[7]McLain and Adams (1937).

[8]Idem.

nounced the holding of Sunday School at 9:00 a.m. and preaching services at 3:00 and 7:00 p.m. Since Emanuel was dividing
his time between a pastorate at Stewart Chapel in Daytona and
St. Paul M.E. Church in New Smyrna, which no longer exists,
one possibly would conclude that services were not held every
Sunday at Stewart. There are suggestions that he might have had
responsibilities in Ormond and Deland, also. In a later column,
he suggested that there was a well developed Sunday School and
Epworth League (Youth League) here as early as 1901. During
the spring of that year, the Florida Conference held its annual
convention at Stewart Chapel.[9]

Figure 3.2: Early members of Stewart Chapel

Who were the early members of Stewart Chapel (Memorial)? Although the lack of written records makes it impossible
to identify the early members, the names of early trustees can
be ascertained from bank transactions. It was through building
and expansion efforts, and the need to secure money for those
purposes, that we learn names of persons identified with the
early church. Among the trustees in 1904 were J.S. Clark, E.W.
Smith, H.C. McLain, R.H. Harris, Joseph Colyer and G..A.
Adams. They were instrumental in the purchase of:

> Lot 24 of Block 1 of Laura E. Walls subdivision of
> Lot 12-13-14 and west 1/3 of lot 11, Block 52 of

---

[9]*Daytona Gazette News*, April 13, 1901.

Mason and Coleman Addition to Daytona.[10]

Additional land was purchased in 1926 from R.S. and Ida A. Maley, when the church acquired lot 18 of the same tract.

Trustees at the time of the purchase included: Texas A. Adams, Mary McLeod Bethune, J.S. Clark, J.D. Gibbs and W.R. Jones.[11] In 1926, Lucille Stephens was secretary and T.A. Adams was treasurer.[12] In 1923, three years earlier, G..E. Riddick was chairman of the Board and J.D. Gibbs was secretary.[13]

During the pastorate of G.B. Lennon, the old structure of Stewart Memorial was razed, and a more pretentious building was begun. While the small congregation was hopeful of quickly constructing a new edifice, the winds of the 1926 hurricane were not cooperative. They blew down the unfinished walls of the future Stewart Memorial. Although this unfortunate incident caused a delay in building a new edifice, a new architectural design was proposed.[14]

In the meantime, the faithful continued to worship, and they were led for a short while by Matthew W. Clair, Jr., a graduate of Howard University who had held pastoral charges in Virginia and West Virginia before being assigned to Stewart Memorial. Later, he was elected Bishop.[15] J.W. Moultrie followed Clair. The next pastor, W.P. Pickens, supervised the revision of the building plan, and devoted his efforts to the completion of the first portion of the old Stewart Memorial, which

---

[10]Trustees of Stewart Chapel Methodist Episcopal Church, Contract with Equitable Building and Loan Company of Daytona, Florida, May 10, 1904.

[11]Stewart Memorial Methodist Episcopal Church, Contract with Merchant Bank and Trust Company, June 1, 1926.

[12]Stewart Memorial M.E. Church Contract with Daytona Bank and Trust Co., January 1, 1926.

[13]H. C. McLain and Dr. T. A. Adams, "Historical Data," The Cele-bration of the Forty-Fourth Anniversary of Stewart Memorial Meth-odist Episcopal Church, December 15-19, 1937, 3.

[14]McLain and Adams (1937).

[15]See Appendix C, biography of Matthew Walker Clair, Jr.

later became the educational building. Other pastors of this period included J.S. Yedd, Thomas A. Huger (father of long-time
member, James E. Huger, Sr.) and J.W. Keller. S.D. Bankston
replaced him, and it was under his pastoral charge that the sanctuary of the old Stewart Memorial was completed.[16] In addition
to the thanks extended to the pastor, congregations and friends
who made the new structure possible, recognition was given to
the valuable contribution of H.W. Bartley, District Superintendent. His dream was to make possible a sanctuary that could
serve the needs of Bethune-Cookman College and the broader
community, as well as the church congregation.[17] He was the
father of the late H.E. Bartley and the grandfather of Muriel J.
Bartley.

Figure 3.3: The First
Sanctuary

Shortly after the completion
of the sanctuary, Harry L.
Burney, Sr. (father of the late
Harry L. Burney, Jr., a long
time member) assumed the
pastorate. A major event that
occurred during his pastoral
charge was the observance of
the 44th anniversary of the
church on December 15-19,
1937. It was a jubilant occasion,
with several events planned
for the celebration, including
Men's and Women's Nights. On Men's Night, S.D. Bankston, a
previous pastor who currently was serving as superintendent of
the Atlantic District of the South Florida Conference, returned
to deliver a brief sermon. Also appearing on the program were
several other speakers, including Texas A. Adam, who spoke on
the subject: "Stewart Memorial's Place in Florida Methodism."
Music was provided by a male choir from Bethune-Cookman
College and the Men's Inter-denominational Choir. Both
groups were significant: the Bethune-Cookman group was
indicative of the close relationship between the college and

---

[16]McLain and Adams (1937).

[17]Historical Statement, Celebration: A Service of Consecration and Open
House, Stewart Memorial United Methodist Church, April 15, 1973.

the church, and the Interdenominational group denoted the church's ecumenical nature.

The Women's Night was equally impressive. Presiding over the occasion was Ladosca Adams (the wife of Texas A. Adams), and appearing on the program were persons who were well known, and active, at the time of the Centennial Observance—Virginia Darby (Fulword), Sarah Bazzell (Burns) and F.L. Dyett (Florence Roane). Other participants included Wilhelmina Colston, Jessie Stephens, Rosalie I. Singleton and Irma Allen. The Bethune-Cookman College female group provided music for the occasion.[18]

From 1937 to 1946, several well-qualified ministers held the pastoral charge at Stewart Memorial, including James L. Todd, C.R.A. Banks, Jerome F. Delpino, A.C. Trice, D.H. McLain and Evan M. Hurley.[19] As was characteristic of the Methodist Church, pastors came and went, but after 1946, Rogers P. Fair, became a rather permanent fixture at Stewart Memorial. Not that he was always pastor, but with the exception of a one-year absence, he was a resident of the city, as an employee of Bethune-Cookman College.

Figure 3.4: Rogers P. Fair

Unlike previous ministerial charges, records exist to document the "Fair era" and later pastorates. Rogers Fair's coming to Stewart Memorial was made possible by the death of C.K. Brown, pastor of Ebenezer Methodist Episcopal Church of Jacksonville, Florida. Evan M. Hurley, who at that time was pastor of Stewart Memorial, was named to replace him, thus

---

[18]The Celebration of the Forty-Fourth Anniversary of Stewart Memorial Methodist Episcopal Church, Souvenir Program, December 15-19, 1937, 5-6.

[19]List of Pastors, Stewart Memorial United Methodist Church, 100th Anniversary Celebration, March, 14, 1993.

leaving a vacancy in its pulpit.[20] Mary McLeod Bethune conducted a search and, with the approval of Texas Adams, the
Methodist Episcopal Church named Fair to replace Hurley. He
assumed the pastoral charge of Stewart Memorial in December
1946.[21]

As pastor, one of the first tasks assumed by Fair was to prepare a handbook that described the ministry of Stewart Memorial. The small booklet described the relationship of the church
to Bethune-Cookman College, listed the administrative officers,
and described the various ministries. In his pastoral statement,
Fair wrote:

> We can no longer talk our religion, for to be a
> Christian we must be active. And this must be
> expressed in terms of what we do. Thus, this little
> book expresses what Stewart Memorial is trying to
> do, and is dedicated to all who might come across
> a copy.[22]

Four ministers served during the interval of Fair's first pastoral charge at Stewart Memorial from 1946-1951 and his second one in 1968-70 including: J.A. Adams, Arthur R. Crowell,
Eddie J. Rivers and Sylvester Gillespie. Following Fair's second
term, William Higgins served until Fair assumed the pastorate
for the third time in 1971.[23]

---

[20]Handbook of Stewart Memorial Methodist Church, 1893-1947, 2-3.

[21]Adewumi Adewale, Dr. Rogers P. Fair: "Bethune-Cookman College's
Most Unforgettable Character," *The Clarion*, Winter 1993, 7.

[22]Handbook of Stewart Memorial Methodist Church, 1893-1947, 1.

[23]Administrative Board Minutes and Historical Statement, 1973.

Chapter 4

Prelude to a New Beginning

Securing a site for a new church building was a major discussion at the April 1, 1968 meeting of the Administrative Board. Following the discussion, a committee, headed by James Huger, was appointed to consider the matter. Other members who were selected for the committee were: W.R. Crooms, Harrison DeShields, Clara Smith and Anthony Stephens.[1] After deliberating, the committee recommended the building of a new sanctuary and supporting units. Once that decision was made, the next issue was the raising of the necessary funds. President Richard V. Moore of Bethune-Cookman College, a proven fund-raiser, was asked to spearhead the effort. Appointed to assist him on the Building Committee were: Harry Burney, Mary Morse, Joseph Smith, James Huger, Florence Roane, president of the Women Society of Christian Service, Joel Fears, president of the Methodist Men, Charles Cherry, W. R. Crooms, president of the Trustees, Theodore Jones, head of the Council of Ministries and Barbara Moore, youth. J. Milburn McLeod, District Superintendent, agreed to be cooperative.[2]

---

[1] Administrative Board Minutes and Historical Statement, April 1, 1968.
[2] AB Minutes and Historical Statement, June 12, 1969.

Once organized, the committee began to look at prospective sites and evaluate their potentials. On June 29, 1969, Moore reported to the Administrative Board that the Building Committee had decided to make an effort to buy a lot, which appeared desirable, if the bid submitted by Stewart Memorial was accepted. He noted that 10% of the asking price must be paid at the time the bid was accepted.[3]

The discussion at the September 29, 1969 Administrative Board meeting centered on hiring an architect and supplying the information needed to begin the work. Even though it appeared that an out-of-town architect could be employed at less cost, the Board seemed to prefer a local firm. In response to the question, "What do we want in a building?" most members appeared to favor a sanctuary that could seat 350 persons, a fellowship hall that could accommodate 125, ten rooms for education, a kitchen, a pastor's study, a reception room, a choir room, a nursery, a lounge, and rest rooms.[4]

While it is always easy to entertain big dreams, the problem of financing them often brings us back to reality. Plans had to be adjusted to what the church could afford to pay. Likewise, the Building Committee had to devise plans by which the building proposal could be financed. Selling existing property, acquiring loans, and raising as much as possible through pledges and rallies were considered.

Richard Moore reported to the October 27, 1969 Administrative Board meeting that he had conferred with the District Superintendent concerning the sale of the property formerly owned by the Methodist Church in Ormond Beach, and the old Trinity Church in the southern part of Daytona Beach.[5] The availability of these properties resulted from the closing of the Methodist churches in those areas because of insufficient members.

Not only was the sale of the property of the old Ormond

---

[3] AB Minutes and Historical Statement, June 29, 1969.
[4] AB Minutes and Historical Statement, September 29, 1969.
[5] AB Minutes and Historical Statement, October 27, 1969.

Beach Methodist feasible to finance the new structure of Stewart Memorial, it was needed to recuperate some of the financial losses suffered in regard to it. Earlier, the pastor and congregation had been informed that the City of Ormond Beach had given Stewart Memorial 30 days to demolish the decayed building, which was a hazard.[6] On November 30, 1970, it was reported that the removal of the debris had cost Stewart Memorial $250.00.[7] After resolving some legal problems, the property was sold.

After it became clear that Stewart Memorial would not relocate to the southern part of Daytona Beach, the church proceeded to put the old Trinity Church up for sale. On January 3, 1972 the Administrative Board authorized the Trustees (with approval of the Conference) to contact a lawyer for the purpose of drawing up a contract for sale of the Trinity Church property. The price was $4,000 with a minimum down payment of $500 to $1,000 and a payment of $50 per month with 6% interest until paid in full, or $3,500 in cash. The old Trinity church was sold to Mt. Moriah Baptist Church.[8] As planned, the old Stewart Memorial also would be sold; however, it still was being used for church services.

Simultaneously, the Building Committee was pursuing gifts and loans, which would be essential in erecting the new building. At the March 30, 1970 Administrative Board meeting, Moore indicated that the church would be able to obtain $3000.00 from the Florida Conference with $1000.00 of that amount as a gift, and $2000.00 as a loan to be paid in five years or so. The Board adopted a resolution thanking Dr. McLeod, District Superintendent for the role he played in the process, and solicited his aid in future efforts.[9]

Moore reported at the April 27, 1970 meeting that "because of the tremendous importance of our church to the college com-

---

[6]AB Minutes and Historical Statement, October 26, 1970.

[7]AB Minutes and Historical Statement, November 30, 1970.

[8]AB Minutes and Historical Statement, January 3, 1972.

[9]AB Minutes and Historical Statement, March 30, 1970.

munity and to Daytona Beach," he was suggesting that Stewart Memorial ask the Church Extension Section of the General Board of Mission for a donation of $20,000 and a loan of $70,000.[10]

While efforts were being made to secure finances externally, similar plans were being pursued internally. Typical of these was the special drive for the building fund, which was held on October 10, 1971 at the chapel of Bethune-Cookman College. A goal of $20,000 was set.[11] Another money-raising endeavor was that of Church Loyalty Sunday, February 20, 1972. Each man was asked to contribute $10.00 and each woman $5.00. Mayor Nathaniel Vereen of Eatonville was the speaker for this occasion.[12]

---

[10]AB Minutes and Historical Statement, April 27, 1970.

[11]Church Bulletin, September 12, 1971.

[12]Church Bulletin, January 30, 1972.

Chapter 5

Realization of a Dream

On May 21, 1972, the groundbreaking ceremonies were held for the new sanctuary. Presiding over these services were Richard V. Moore, chairman of the Building Committee. After some historic glances by Rogers P. Fair, the pastor, words of dedication and the challenge were given by Walter B. Rutland, District Superintendent. Other participants on the program included Eddie J. Rivers, Jr., minister of Tyler

Figure 5.1: Groundbreaking

Temple United Methodist Church of Tampa; Theodore T. Jones, chairman of the Council of Ministries; W.R. Crooms, chairman of the Board of Trustees; John H. Gainey, chairman of the Administrative Board; Shirley Watts (Bing) musician; and A.B. Gallaway, minister of Community United Methodist Church.[1]

Groundbreaking did not assure a completed structure. There was still money to be raised, and other steps to be taken before moving into the new sanctuary. Rallies continued to be held,

---

[1]Groundbreaking Ceremonies For the Proposed Stewart Memorial United Methodist Church , May, 21, 1972.

and the Little White Church collections continued to be taken.[2]

On July 30, 1972 Stewart Memorial observed Family and Friends' Day. Each member was requested to bring a friend and each family was asked to raise a minimum of one hundred dollars.[3] Later, on November 19, 1972, a building fund effort was held and each adult member was asked to raise $100.00.[4]

As January brought in the new year it also brought rising hope. A fellowship hour was held in the new Fellowship Hall of the new church on January 7, 1973. Members and friends were invited to eat, chat, and tour the edifice.[5]

Services of praise and thanksgiving were held in the new sanctuary on March 18, 1973. The congregation joined in singing and in praying prayers of thanksgiving. Fair, the pastor, issued challenges of the new venture, and Richard V. Moore, lay leader, John Gainey, chair of the Administrative Board, and Wealthy Crooms, chair of the Trustee Board also brought greetings.[6]

Figure 5.2: The Building Today

On March 25, the first regular morning services were conducted with Richard Moore, charge lay leader, presiding. The congregation opened the services with singing "Holy, Holy, Holy." Among the activities of this first service was the installing ritual of the new acolyte program, which was planned by Nathalie Jenkins.[7]

Approximately a month later, Sunday, April 15, 1973, a joyous congregation assembled to dedicate the new structure (the present one), which consisted of a sanctuary, kitchen, a fellowship hall /dining room narthex, pastor's study, choir room and sacristy.

In the souvenir program for the occasion, Fair wrote:

There is always a tinge of sadness when we desert

[2] See church bulletin for first Sunday of each month in 1972.
[3] Church Bulletin, July 23, 1972.
[4] Church Bulletin, October 1, 1972.
[5] Church Bulletin, January 7, 1973.

the old for the new. The saints of yesteryear, both lay-persons and ministers, will never vacate our memories, and we shall take with us a history pregnant with magnificent moments of both message and mission. Our moving into the new will constitute no break in our historical chain. It will merely indicate our growth and maturity under the direction of the Holy Spirit.[8]

The booklet honored the memories of Lucille Warren Stephens and Texas A. Adams, "whose dedication and unselfish service to Christ and His church made possible the building of both the old and new Stewart Memorial United Methodist Church."[9]

Memorial Gifts

As an expression of gratitude, some members and friends made gifts to the new church. The following contributed sanctuary pews and other gifts.

Sanctuary Pews

Adams (The Family of the late Dr. Texas A. Adams)
Barnes, Mr. and Mrs. Frank
Bartley, Dr. and Mrs., Henry E.
Burney, Mr. and Mrs. Harry L., Jr.
Christian, Mrs. Henry
Crooms, Mrs. W.R.
DeShields, Mr. and Mrs. Harrison L
Edwards, Mr. and Mrs. Albert
Fulword, Mrs. Virginia
Gainey, Mr. and Mrs. John
Gibbs, Mrs. Margaret
Irvin, Mr. and Mrs. Bernard

---

[8] Stewart Memorial United Methodist Church, 100th Anniversary Celebration, March 14, 1993.

[9] Idem.

Jenkins, Mr. and Mrs. C.W.

Jones, Mrs. Lucile

Kornegay, Dr. and Mrs. William

Miller, Mrs. Jerona and Daughter

Morse, Miss Mary

McLendon, Mrs. Hazeleen

Nicholson, Mr. and Mrs. Theodore

Pierce, Mr. William

Rodriguez, Mr. Edward G..

Stephens, Dr. Anthony J. and Hogan, Mrs. Dorothy

Other Gifts

Curinton, Mrs. Flossie: 150-piece Place Setting (Dining Area)

Doelger, Mrs. Willie Mae: Two Multi-Purpose Tables

Fair, Reverend and Mrs. Rogers P.: Pulpit and Pulpit Chair

Gainous, Jr. Dr. and Mrs. Rabbie J., Jr.: Electric Stove for Kitchen

Greene, Mr. and Mrs. J. Griffen: Communion Rail

Greene, Mrs. James: Reception Room Furniture

Harris, Mrs. Dufferin: Baptismal Font

Huger, Dr. and Mrs. James E.: Interior, Rough Hewn Cross (Sanctuary)

Moore, Dr. and Mrs. Richard V.: Electric Refrigerator for Kitchen

Roane, Dr. Florence L.: Lectern

Shears, Mr. C. S.: Vacuum Cleaner

Slaughter, Mrs. Gwendolyn: Electric Coffee Urn

Temple, Mr. and Mrs. Lawrence: The Christian Flag

Webb, Mr. Joseph: 100 Chairs for Fellowship Hall

Webb, Mrs. Joseph: Complete Altar Set

The Ushers Board, Mrs. Albert Edwards, President: Outside Bulletin Board

The Young, Active Christians of Stewart (YACS): Piano[10]

---

[10]Idem.

Even though the new structure had been dedicated, there remained a few more rituals to be performed. One was the laying of the cornerstone. That event took place on May 13, 1973 in special services in which Rudolph Matthew, pastor of Mount Bethel Baptist Institutional Church was the main speaker. The laying of the cornerstone was performed by Masonic leaders from throughout Florida. A fellowship dinner followed, which was prepared by a committee headed by Juanita Sharper and Thelma Hall.[11]

With the disposal of church property in southern Daytona Beach and Ormond and the announcement by Charles Cherry that an agreement had been reached concerning the purchase of the old Stewart Memorial for $21,850, the church was motivated to conduct a few more rallies and finally reached the point where there was no payment left on the mortgage. That, indeed, was a time for rejoicing. The members were equally happy to learn that the old Stewart Memorial would become the Richard V. Moore Center, named in honor of the church's lay leader.[12]

Encouraged by a gift from the Burrows/McZier Families, the Rosa Burrows Room, which houses the library and prayer corner, became an addition to Stewart Memorial in 1980. The garage also was added that year.

Full of joy were the members of Stewart Memorial on April 5, 1981 when they celebrated "the Burning of the Mortgage" in a Service of Thanksgiving and Holy Communion. Being celebrated were the final payment on a loan acquired for the purpose of constructing the new sanctuary. Leading this celebration was Bishop Earl G. Hunt, Jr. of the

Figure 5.3: The Burning of the Mortgage

Florida Conference (UMC), William M. Ferguson, Superintendent of the Deland District (FCUMC) and Rogers P. Fair, pastor.

---

[11]Church Bulletin, May 6, 1973.

[12]Administrative Board Minutes and Historical Statement, August 29, 1975.

Other participants included Shirley Watts Bing, organist; James
E. Huger, church business manager; Richard V. Moore, charge
lay leader; Joel Fears, chairperson of the Administrative Board;
Florence L. Roane, certified lay speaker; Lucien Lewis, soloist;
George Whitehead, chairperson Committee of Finance; Oswald
P. Bronson, president of Bethune-Cookman College; Wealthy
Crooms, chairperson of the Board of Trustees; Franklin Boston,
vice chairman of the Board of Trustees; and Albert Edwards.
The Chancel Choir provided music.[13]

The next big event at Stewart Memorial was the retirement
of Rogers P. Fair, who had served the church for twenty-eight
years. On April 14, 1986, the church and community said
"thank you" to Fair at a retirement dinner at the Daytona
Hilton Hotel. The elaborate affair was attended by city and
county officials, Methodist leaders of the Deland District,
college officials, and numerous people from the ministerial,
business, and civic communities, and of course, almost all of
the members of Stewart Memorial.

In a written statement, Earl Hunt, Jr., resident bishop of the
Florida Conference lauded him as thus:

> There is no way to measure the far-reaching in-
> fluence of your illustrious ministry upon Florida
> Methodism. Your splendid leadership in both the
> Central Jurisdiction and the Florida Conference of
> the Southeastern Jurisdiction has been most signifi-
> cant, and will be felt for generations yet to come. [14]

A second retirement celebration was held at the church, pri-
marily for the members of Stewart Memorial. They wanted to
say thanks for the many achievements that had been made dur-

[13]The Burning of the Mortgage in a Service of Thanksgiving and Holy
Communion, April 5, 1981.

[14]The Stewart Memorial United Methodist Church Family and Friends Retirement Dinner Honoring the Doctor Rogers Pressley Fair, Sr., at Daytona
Hilton Hotel, April 14, 1986. 15 p. 4.

ing his tenure—a new sanctuary and supporting units, an improved musical program, new ministries, and a substantial increase in membership. With his retirement, he served as a supply pastor for Trinity United Methodist Church in St Augustine. Although, he was no longer pastor of Stewart Memorial, he was always a part of it, and he returned on many occasions.

Fair was succeeded by Eddie J. Rivers, Jr., a former pastor of Stewart Memorial, and superintendent of Sarah Hunt Methodist Children's Home. Although his tenure was short-lived because of his pending retirement, he maintained good rapport with the congregation. As a musician, he maintained an active interest in the musical program of the church—often performing or directing. Even though he retired from Stewart Memorial, and went through the retirement rituals, he did not cease to be a part of it. He continued to visit the ill, counsel those who needed it, and funeralize those whose families requested. Rivers' second tenure was from 1986-1990. Afterwards, he accepted the post of supply pastor of Trinity United Methodist Church in Sanford, FL.

Alfonso Delaney, a student of Rogers P. Fair, replaced Eddie J. Rivers. His tenure also was short, due to his appointment to the pastoral charge of Ebenezer in Miami. Carrill S. Munnings replaced him, leaving his pastoral charge in Clearwater to do so. He was serving at the time of the Centennial Observance.

Chapter 6

Celebrating a Centennial

"Rejoice! We Love Thy Church O God," was the theme for the centennial celebration at Stewart Memorial United Methodist Church. While none of the original members were present to celebrate this joyous occasion, fifteen members who had held church membership for more than fifty years either joined in the observance, or were there in spirit. Fifty-year members included:

Bertha Baker, 83

Margaret Bartley, 56

Palmsy Smith, 68

Thelma Hall, 55

Ruth E. Neal, 63

Juanita Sharper, 55

Dorothy L. Perkins, 63

Lorenza Gamble, 54

Virginia Fulword, 58

Eloise Edwards Snell, 54

Eunice Pettway, 58

Phannye B. Huger, 51

James E. Huger, Sr., 56

Beatrice Rowe, 50

Sarah B. Burns, 56

Those who had served more than twenty-five years at Stewart Memorial also were recognized. They were:

Mable Jackson, 49

Carrie C. Blevins, 37

Delores B. Davis, 48

Annie M. Bell, 36

Hazeleen McLendon, 48

Delia Way, 36

Dorothy S. Hogan, 47

John L. Huger, 35

Richard V. Moore, 45

Gladys Greene, 34

B. J. Moore, 44

Shirley Watts-Bing, 33

Willie Mae Doelger, 43

Teresa Davis, 33

Margaret Gibbs, 42

John R. Heath, 34

Mable D. Christian, 42

Donthel Hall, 30

Henry T. Christian, 42

Maxine A. Temple, 29

Luvert G. Roberson, 40

Minnie J. Harris, 29

N. Crooms Jenkins, 40

Sadie S. Stephens, 28

Olga L. Thompson, 39

Joel V. Fears, Sr., 25

Charles W. Cherry, 39

Celestine D. Hinson, 25

Julia T. Cherry, 39

Shirley Moore, 25

Hortense M. Mathis, 38

S Louise Rosemond, 25

Charles W. Mathis, 37

Hercules Swilley, 25

On this historic occasion, Donald F. Padgett, District Superintendent for the Deland District of the United Methodist Church, observed:

> You are indeed one of the strongest churches in our
> Florida Conference. We are grateful for the way
> you have led the Daytona community in many wor-
> thy projects for Christ across the years, and for the
> meaningful way you have always been involved in
> the life of Bethune-Cookman College.[1]

In noting that it was a significant milestone for the church, Bishop H. Hasbrouck Hughes, Jr. observed: "Stewart Memorial is among our great churches, and its witness across the years is well known."[2]

Rev. & Mrs. Carrill S. Munnings, Sr., in their congratulatory remarks wrote: "May your next century of ministry be as vibrant as your first has been. Keep your lamps trimmed and

---

[1] Stewart Memorial United Methodist Church, 100th Anniversary Celebration, March 14, 1993.

[2] Ibid.

burning with the oil of gladness and readiness to serve." It was during the tenure of Carrill Munnings that we celebrated the end of the first hundred years, and launched into the second hundred.

The centennial sermon was delivered by Rogers P. Fair, the former pastor of Stewart Memorial and chaplain of Bethune-Cookman College. Of all the pastors, he served the longest charge—twenty-eight years.

The centennial observance was a time to recall the progress of the church since its founding, especially the comfort afforded the worshippers. Bertha Baker, whose membership dates back to 1910, was present in all the places of worship. She worshipped in the Stewart Chapel, the old Stewart Memorial and the current edifices. Likewise, she witnessed the change in name from Stewart Memorial Methodist Episcopal to Stewart Memorial Methodist, and finally to Stewart Memorial United Methodist. Other members also can recall the many changes over the first centennial.

Like many other churches, Stewart Memorial was the scene of many hours of sadness, as funerals in abundance were held to say good-by to fellow Churchmen. It was also the setting for moments of happiness as fellow-members took their wedding vows in the sanctuary of Stewart Memorial. Many of their children were baptized in the church.

In 1993, choirs and the congregation were continuing to sing such historic hymns as "Holy! Holy! Holy," "O Worship the King," and "O for a Thousand Tongues to Sing" and such spirituals as "Come Out the Wilderness," and "Nobody Knows the Trouble I've Seen." It is hard to believe that these well-known songs were not among those utilized by Stewart Memorial in 1893, the year of its founding. Likewise, scriptures like the 23rd, 27th, 46th, and 100th Psalms are continuing to provide inspiration for the congregation today.

The Centennial celebration was important to Stewart Memorial since it gave the congregation the opportunity to revisit the past, considering both its successes and failures. Simultaneously, it enabled the church to anticipate its future

more accurately. Hopefully, the decision was made to make the
next one hundred years more rewarding.

Chapter 7

The Second Century

Carrill Munnings, whose duty it was as pastor to end the first century and to begin the second, expressed satisfaction with the centennial observance, and challenged the congregation to meet the needs of the second hundred years. While there was much to celebrate during the first century, there remained some nagging problems to be resolved. Throughout most of the history of the church there were problems of finance, youth activities and low attendance at such functions as the church school, prayer meeting and other activities. A major challenge then was how to find solutions to these problems. The church, in compliance with its Mission Statement set out to adopt new approaches. The statement reads:

> The mission and ministry of this church is to be a concerned, faithful and caring community reaching out to all. It is the purpose of each witness herein to disperse God's love and gospel throughout our community in Christian activities as well as through daily living.[1]

---

[1] Stewart Memorial United Methodist Church, 100th Anniversary Celebration, March 14, 1993, 10.

After a six-month study and exploration, the Vision 2000 committee issued its report on July 12, 1993. Based on a survey of church members and participation of the committee in four intensive workshops, seven major priorities were listed. They are ranked in order of importance:

- Priority #1: To Reach Out.

- Priority #2: To Intentionally Invite.

- Priority #3: To Revise Sunday School. (Our Christian Education in general needs revising to include new audio/visual teaching helps such as video tape).

- Priority #4: To Increase our Stewardship through a Small Group Ministry of Christian nurture and spiritual discipline."

- Priority #5: To develop our Youth Ministries.

- Priority #6: To set up a nursery.

- Priority #7: To build for more classroom space.

The Committee recommended that priorities #1, #2, and #3 be implemented with the acceptance of the report. It noted that, "the completion of this part of our church's vision is a must for the consideration of the other four priorities." The Committee referred to several suggested activities discussed in their various sessions. They included:

- Reaching Out to the Unchurched

- Being an Inviting Church

- Wesley Small Groups Ministry

- Youth Ministry[2]

---

[2]"Vision 2000 Document," July 12, 19, 1.

Among specific activities, it suggested:

> marketing the church through the offering of 'free'
> or discounted services like the SHARE Food Co-op
> or baby sitting for a day, establishing and distribut-
> ing a church brochure, developing a ministry of
> friendship (even a 'Celebration of Friendship Day'
> in which we would honor our friends in the com-
> munity), enhancing our hospitality ministry to visi-
> tors by having members wear "name tags,' placing
> 'visitors' parking spaces next to the pastor's space,
> greeting members in the parking lot (not just at the
> door) and calling visitors within 24 hours of their
> visit."[3]

Although not designated as Friendship Day, the Women's
Day Committee chose to pay tribute to one hundred women of
the community in its observance for 2000.[4]

In April 1995, Munnings assured the church that "Vision
2000 is well under way." In the attempt to achieve some of
its basic goals, he talked with the owner of the adjacent property to ascertain whether he might be interested in selling it.
Munnings expressed hope that the church could "build an educational wing that will 'double' as a daycare." He appealed
to the Finance and Pastor Parrish Relations Committee to "help
us in reaching our youth for Christ" He stated his interest in the
employment of a youth minister "to jump start and bolster a new
and vital youth programmed ministry (Youth Program, UMYF,
Youth Choir and Youth Sunday School)."[5]

Much of the vision was continued under the pastoral charge
of Joreatha Capers. Consistent with the Wesley small group
Ministries, Capers proposed sending a team to Atlanta, Georgia
on July 6-8, 1995 to attend a disciple seminar to prepare Stewart

---

[3] Administrative Board, April 30, 2000.
[4] Pastor's Report of April 5, 1995.
[5] Idem.

Memorial for the launching of a Disciple Bible Ministry. *Disciple* is defined as "a program of disciplined Bible study aimed at developing strong Christian leaders. [It] focuses on the disciple as learner, believer, follower, proclaimer, servant." In addition to the pastor, Joreatha Capers, those who attended the seminar were Sallie Shelton Culver, Cleo Higgins, Sheila Flemming, Lynn Thompson, Michelle Thompson, and Margaret Watson.[6] In recalling the trip to Atlanta, Culver wrote:

> It was a warm and humid summer night Wednesday July 5, 1995 when eight of us began our trip to Atlanta, Georgia for Disciple Training. I fell asleep shortly after the trip started. When I awaken, the church van was parked at a convenience store on Interstate By-pass 295 near Jacksonville, Florida. Dr. Capers, our pastor, and others were concerned that "we just can not get the van started and the people in the store will not let us in," at 1:30 a.m. on Thursday. Their policy was to continue selling gas, but not allow anyone into the store "after hours."[7]

The potential disciples were able to make the trip to Atlanta, attend the seminar, and return to Stewart Memorial and organize its first disciple program in 1995.

Also introduced at the church were the Contemporary Worship Service, BCC Freshmen Orientation Booth, Grief Ministry, and a Youth Fellowship Enhancement. Contemporary Worship Services were held at 8:00 a.m., and it appealed to those who did not like to worship the traditional way, and those who wanted to do other things later in the day. Lynn Thompson was placed in charge of the early morning services. Many student-ministers were used in the Contemporary Services. The B-CC Freshmen Orientation Booth did much to strengthen relations between the

---

[6]"Continuing Education Report of Minister and Laity, Third and Fourth Quarter," October 9, 1995.

[7]*Disciple: Our Story*, 1997, p. 2.

church and college, and in the meantime, it directed many students to Stewart Memorial for regular worship during the year. The Youth Fellowship Enhancement Program under the leadership of Cleo Higgins and Jake Miller provided a variety of activities for the youth, but they were never organized into the United Methodist Youth Fellowship, as anticipated.[8]

In 1996, an administrative council re-organization plan was introduced as a means of revitalizing the church. The reorganization plan resulted from a report by a committee composed of Sallie Shelton Culver, chair of the Administrative Council, Joel Fears and Minnie Harris who, along with Gladys Greene visited First United Methodist Church in Port Orange, and First United Methodist Church of Ormond. They made the following recommendations, which later were approved by the Administrative Board and the Charge Conference. The organizational structure did away with the Council on Ministry, and grouped its activities into five ministries: Outreach, Nurture and Caring, Worship, Growth and Enrichment, and Events.[9]

In 1996, Capers left Stewart Memorial to accept the position of assistant general secretary of the "United Methodist Church Black College Fund and Ethnic Concerns." She was replaced with Kevin James, the chaplain of Bethune-Cookman. During his two-year tenure, 1996-1998, progress continued in the various ministries. He showed a special interest in the church school. Stewart Memorial rejoiced in his being elevated to the post of superintendent of the St. Petersburg District. Michael Frazier succeeded him both as pastor of Stewart Memorial and chaplain of Bethune-Cookman College.

During his tenure, the church continued to search for meaningful reform. In 1998, William Jefferson Smith (youth) and Andy Jackson, Sr. represented Stewart Memorial at the Florida/Atlanta Connection. The theme of this seminar, held at Ben Hill United Methodist Church in Decatur, GA, was

---

[8] Youth Fellowship
[9] Administrative Board *Action News*, July 15, 1996.

"Increasing Membership Among African Americans." Jackson reported that the major points given to increase membership of churches were:

- Adapt to people's schedule (i.e. offer different times/days for worship services),

- Advertise,

- Involve the whole congregation in solving problems within the church,

- Provide plenty of recreational activities and social gatherings for the youth.[10]

In the Lay Leader Report to the Administrative Council in July1998, Sheila Flemming noted the reaction of the church membership to the appointment of a pastor whose work was divided between the church and Bethune-Cookman College. The consensus of the approximately 100 people who attended the meeting was that we should prepare to ask for a full-time pastor at the next Charge Conference.[11]

A more important phase of her report was for the Administrative Council to brainstorm about the vision of the church as it relates to programs and space. She also recommended that the Council appoint a Long-Term Planning Committee. She suggested James Huger as chair, and members Sallie Shelton Culver, Jake Miller, Collace Greene, Joel Fears, Minnie Harris, Samuel Sharper, Sheila Flemming and a youth representative.[12]

The Long-Term Planning Committee was asked to: (a) review the "Vision 2000" report, (b) consider the brainstorming ideas of the July 6th meeting, (c) include deliberation and possibilities for new and expanded programs for the church, (d) include well thought out plans for space expansion for the church,

---

[10] *The Vine*, Vol. 10, July 1998.

[11] "Lay Leader Report," Administrative Council, July 6, 1998.

[12] "Lay Leader's Recommendations for Long Range Planning Committee," Administrative Council, July 6, 1998.

including consultation with an architect, and (e) any other goals and works desired by the Administrative Council.[13]

The Long-Range Planning Committee, chaired by James Huger, was composed of three sub-committees: Programs and Ministries Committee chaired by Lynn Thompson, Building and Space Committee headed by Collace Greene, and Funding Task Committee chaired by Toni Stewart.

In its evaluations of the ministries of the church, the Committee on Programs and Ministries concluded that:

> The key to attracting new members is first by re-energizing many of our existing members and developing new approaches to making the worship experience on Sundays so attractive that we can involve more people in other events that happen during the week.

Perceiving "a fresh approach to the worship experience" as essential to the growth of the congregation, the committee recommended workshops for worship leaders, choir members and musicians. As it related to worship services, it was suggested that it might be necessary to employ additional musicians to change the musical phase of worship "in an aggressive and attractive fashion."[14]

The Outreach Ministry was seen as meeting the needs of the church, but too few people are involved in the actual implementation of the ministry. It was concluded that the Ministry of Nurture and Caring was performing its job well as it relates to children, young people, seniors and health and welfare issues, but it was suggested that, "class leaders can be more effective in terms of spiritual guidance." It was recognized however, that there was a need for more people to be involved. The Growth and Enrichment and Events Ministries were perceived as needing greater involvement.[15]

---

[13]"Lay Leader Report," Administrative Council, July 6, 1998.
[14]Church Expansion Chair Committee Meeting, August 17, 1998.
[15]Ibid.

The Building and Space Committee, chaired by Collace Greene recommended the extension of the present structure to add a gymnatorium (combined gym and auditorium), choir stand, pastor's office, waiting room and lounge, secretary office, commercial kitchen, rest rooms, additional room, choir stand, and elevator. The second floor would include a choir room and nursery. Relative to the present structure, the committee recommended the elimination of storage room and enlargement of restrooms, the garage to be organized storage space, the Rosa Brooks room to become a reading room/library, and the current fellowship hall be divided for classroom use.[16]

The Funding Task Committee, headed by Toni Stewart, recommended four sources of money: (1) commitment from pledging, (2) commitment from the conference and grants (3) commitment from the bank, and (4) renting the gymnatorium.[17]

In the months that followed, the initial report of the building committee was modified with the gymnatorium being eliminated. With a pledge system designed, the congregation and friends set out to raise the money necessary to make the "wing of faith" a success.

Eddie J. Rivers, who had served two previous terms as pastor (1955-1961 and 1986-1990) was called out of retirement to assume the pastoral charge in 2004. Upon his return, he continued to serve the congregation as a shepherd serves his flock. This service, however, extended to more than his congregation at Stewart Memorial. The Volusia County-Daytona Beach Branch of the NAACP in presenting him a religious leadership award in 2003, acknowledged that he was "considered a community shepherd not only to his own denomination, but also to all who need spiritual assistance in their lives."[18] On June 26 2005, he preached his final sermon at Stewart Memorial before

---

[16]Ibid.

[17]Ibid.

[18]Volusia County - Daytona Beach NAACP 2003, 30th Annual Freedom Fund and Awards Banquet April 25, 2003, 36.

his final retirement. He died July 9, 2005.[19]

In July 2005, Stewart Memorial reached another level when it was assigned a full-time pastor. Walter E. Monroe, the previous pastor of University United Methodist Church of Gainesville, Florida was named its pastor. At the 2006 Charge Conference, Monroe listed three major goals, which he was seeking to reach: an increase of at least 12% in stewardship, an increase in membership of 5%, and the affirmation and support of the historical relationship between Stewart Memorial United Methodist Church and Bethune-Cookman College. He also suggested focusing on his vision statement: "Where Christ, Campus and Community Meet to Grow in Christ."[20]

A change in the administrative order took place during the early years of Monroe's tenure. He organized an Executive Leadership Team, which he described as being like "an executive board," and "accountable to the Administrative Council and Charge Conference."[21] It is composed of the pastor, charge lay leader, chair and secretary of the Administrative Council, chairs of the Staff-Pastor Committee, Finance Committee, Trustee Board, Worship Committee and three at-large members. The members in 2006 were:

Carolyn Solomon, chair; Walter E. Monroe, Jr., pastor; Joel V. Fears, Sr., lay leader; Sedrick Harris, Cal Greene, Franklin Boston; Ralph Solomon, Delores Davis, S. Louise Rosemond, and Harold Heard.[22]

In regard to its functions, the pastor offers this description:

> The primary task of the team (E.L.T.) will be
> to provide another avenue to discuss important
> issues before they are presented to the Adminis-
> trative Council, to listen to concerns, suggestions,

---

[19]Funeral Program for the Reverend Dr. Eddie James Rivers, Jr., January 15, 2005.

[20]Dr. Walter Monroe, Pastor's Report, 2006 Charge Conference.

[21]Dr. Walter Monroe, Pastor's Report, 2005 Charge Conference.

[22]Program Calendar and Membership Directory, 2007.

and recommendations before official actions are taken.[23]

On August 25-26, 2006, a refocused living retreat was held at Stewart Memorial. Church leaders were introduced to a "two- phase revitalization process that integrates the personal renewal of leaders with the revitalization of their churches." The church leaders, who attended the refocusing retreat were under the leadership of Monroe. "In addition to the retreat, the pastor will be involved in five monthly network meetings and an on-going coaching for pastors' seminar. Likewise, congregation leaders will engage in six follow-up meetings."[24]

In 2006, Stewart Memorial took definitive steps toward making its "Wing of Faith" project a reality. According to Collace C. Greene, chair of the Finance Committee, the first phase of the campaign ended successfully, "resulting in an attractive cash-on hand position to move forward with the follow-on activities." The total raised from pledges of members and friends, funds generated through Conference grant, and personal donations for selected items, made it easier to acquire the necessary credit. The projected funds available is near the required amount needed to undertake "the repair/renovations to the existing building and the design and engineering phase of the new "Wing of Faith" addition."[25] The proposed financial plan was approved by the Administrative Council and the East Central District (FC) of the United Methodist Church. Planned renovations include re-roofing the existing facilities, structural repairs to exterior walls, interior painting, re-carpeting, and removal of air conditioning units in the office areas and library.[26]

[23] Monroe, Pastor's Report, 2005.
[24] "Introducing Refocusing Networks," no date, but used for August 25-26 retreat.
[25] Stewart Memorial United Methodist Church Trustee Board, The Building Committee, October 23, 2006.
[26] "East Central District UMC Approves 'Wing' Project," *Good News Journal* Vol. 1, Issue 1, January 2007.

In 2006, a new ministerial structure was introduced with ministries falling under the following umbrellas: Nurture and Care, Outreach, Witness and Leadership Development and Resource.[27] Likewise, the church continued to evaluate its mission statement, which has been in use for more than a decade.

---

[27]"Welcome to Our Church" brochure.

Chapter 8

Its Administrative Organization

Throughout its existence, Stewart Memorial has had several forms of governmental structures. When the church was young and struggling, little was needed other than a pastor, secretary, treasurer, and a few stewards. As the church began to grow, however, the members perceived a need for expanded programs and facilities, and that required a more sophisticated organization.

The lack of adequate records makes it impossible to identify all early officers, however, names of trustees are available through bank records. J. S. Clark, E. W. Smith, H. C. McLain and G. A. Adams are identified as trustees in 1904.[1] By 1923 G. E. Riddick was chairman of the Board and J. D. Gibbs was secretary.[2] Three years later we could identify the names of two persons who would have an impact on the church for the next two or three decades: Texas A. Adams treasurer and Lucille

---

[1]Contract between Trustees of Stewart Memorial Methodist Episcopal Church (Colored) and The Equitable Building and Loan Company, May 10, 1904.

[2]Contract between Stewart Memorial M.E. Church and Daytona Bank & Trust Company, October 30, 1923.

Stephens, secretary.[3]

Trustees of that year and the next included: Texas A. Adams, James H. Anderson, Mary McLeod Bethune, J. S. Clark, J. D. Gibbs and W. R. Jones.[4]

By 1947, Stewart Memorial had an official board consisting of fourteen stewards, nine trustees and seven other major officers. The stewards were:

J.H. Anglin	Mai Crawford	Shelly Smith
H.E. Bartley	Thomas Graham	Cleo Trapp
L.R. Brassell	Alphonso Jones	E.P. Trapp
E.N. Brown	J.L. Slack	
D.C. Colbert	Joseph Smith	

The trustees were:

T.A. Adams	Alphonso Jones	M. Singleton
H.E. Bartley	O.J. Latimore	E. P. Trapp
L.R. Braswell	R.V. Moore	Edward Van Pool[5]

Other major offices were: James Huger, the chairman of the Local Board of Education; and Margaret Bartley, the chairman of the Board of Mission and Church Extension. Among the officers who reported to the Local Board of Education were: J.L. Slack, superintendent of the Sunday School; T.A. Adams, the lay leader; Selena Clemons, president, women Society of Christian Service; T.A. Adams, president of the Methodist Men; and Mary Alice Cook (Smith), head of the Youth Division. Under the Board of Missions and Extensions were the financial secretary (Katherine Thomas), and treasurer (H.E. Bartley).[6]

---

[3]Contract, April 28, 1926.

[4]Contract between Stewart Memorial Methodist Episcopal Church and Merchant Bank and Trust Company, June 1, 1926 and October 4, 1927.

[5]Handbook of Stewart Memorial Methodist Church, 1893-1947, 4-5.

[6]Ibid., 5.

A church would not be complete without its musical and ushering programs. Anthony Stephens was president of the Senior Choir and Olivia Jones was its organist. Willie Mae Mobley was president of the Junior Choir and Wynona Brown was its organist. E.P. Trapp and his fellow ushers provided the church with a well-organized ushering program.[7]

The organization of 1967 reflected many changes, but it included many of the same personnel. Among the offices which had church-wide responsibilities were: pastor Arthur Crowell, charge lay leader Richard V. Moore, chair of the Administrative Board J. Griffen Greene, treasurer Agnes Fair, chair of the Council on Ministry Theodore Jones, and chair of the Board of Trustees W.R. Crooms.

Among the commissions reporting to the Administrative Board were: Commission on Nominations, Commission on Pastoral Relations, Commission on Membership and Evangelism, Commission on Education (Margaret Bartley), Commission on Missions, Commission on Stewardship and Finance (James Huger), Commission on Social Christian Concern, Commission on Wills & Legacies, Hospital and Home Stewards, Commission on Worship. Building Committee (R. V. Moore, Sr.), class leaders, Parsonage Committee (C. S. Curinton), president of Methodist Men's Club (Harrison DeShields), and a lay delegate to the Annual Conference.[8]

Major officers in 1973 consisted of :

Pastor, Rogers P. Fair

Charge Lay Leader, R. V. Moore, Sr.

Chairman of Administrative Board, John Gainey

Chair of Finance Committee, William Kornegay

Church Treasurer, Agnes Fair

Church Business Manager, James Huger

Financial Secretary, C. W. Jenkins

Superintendent of Study Program, Margaret Bartley

---

[7]Ibid., 8,9.

[8]Administrative Council, April 25, 1967.

Chair of Board of Trustees, W. R. Crooms
Chair of Council of Ministries, Theodore T. Jones
Chair of Pastor-Parish Relations, J. Griffen Greene[9]
In 1998, the chief officers were:
Pastor, Kevin James
Charge Lay Leader, Shelia Flemming
Associate Charge Lay Leader, Bernard Irvin
Chairperson of the Administrative Council, Andy Jackson
Vice Chairperson of the Administrative Council, George Whitehead
Secretary Administrative Council & Charge Lay Leader, Pinkie B. Oliver
Chairperson, Committee on Pastor-Parish Relations, Ralph B. Solomon, Jr.
Chairperson, Board of Trustees, Franklin D. Boston
Chairperson, Committee on Finance, Toni D. Stewart
Financial Secretary, Lucy Heath
Church Treasurer, Samuel Sharper, Sr.
Church Membership Secretary, Lucy Heath
Associate Membership Secretary, Thelma Hall[10]

In 2006, the internal administrative structure had as its base the Administrative Council, headed by Carolyn Solomon. The Administrative Council's chairperson is elected by the Charge Conference annually and is responsible for leading the council in the fulfillment of its responsibilities. "He/she reviews and assigns responsibility for the implementation of actions taken by the council. The council chair provides the initiative and leadership for the council as it does the planning, establishing of objectives and goals and evaluating."[11] Others who have held the office since 1967 are: J. Griffen Greene, Harrison DeShields, John Gainey, John Heath, James Greene, Joel Fears, Bernard

[9] Stewart Memorial United Methodist Church,100th Anniversary Celebration, March 14, 1993, 27-29.
[10] Program Calendar and Membership Directory, 1998.
[11] The Book of Discipline of the United Methodist Church, 1996, 253.3.

Irvin, Collace Greene, Sallie Shelton-Culver (the first lady to hold the position), Andy Jackson, and Carolyn Solomon.[12]

Included among the major administrative officers is the church treasurer, a position that few have held during Stewart Memorial's more than one hundred year history. An early church document indicates that Texas A. Adams was treasurer in 1926,[13] and a later document revealed that H.E. Bartley was serving in that position in 1946.[14] J.S. Slacks served as treasurer prior to the tenure of Agnes Fair, which extended from 1958 to 1986.[15] She was replaced by Samuel Sharper, Sr., who in 2007 is continuing to serve as treasurer.[16]

In 2006, Lucy Heath served the church as financial secretary, as she had done for several years. Persons who have previously served in that position include: Lucille Stephens, Cornelius Jenkins, Dorothy Hogan and Wilnette O'Rourke.[17] Lucy Heath also served as membership secretary. Minnie Harris was her assistant, and Delores Davis was the recording secretary for the Administrative Council.[18]

The *Book of Discipline* also provides for a committee on pastor-parish relations, committee on finance, committee of lay leadership, and a board of trustees.[19] In 2006, the Committee on Pastor-Parish Relations was chaired by Ralph Solomon, and its members, according to classes, were:

Class of 2006	Class of 2007	Class of 2008
Gladys Greene	Collace Greene, Sr.	Sallie Shelton Culver
John Heath	Mary Alice Smith	Delores Davis
Wanda Pride	Ralph Solomon	D'John Greer[20]

---

[12]Administrative Council Minutes.
[13]Contract, April 28, 1926.
[14]Handbook of Stewart Memorial Methodist Church, 1893-1947, 5.
[15]Information provided by Mrs. Agnes Fair.
[16]Membership Directories.
[17]Contract, April 28, 1926 and Membership Directories.
[18]Church Officers, 2006.
[19]The Book of Discipline of the United Methodist Church, 1996, 246.
[20]Church Officers 2006.

Consistent with the discipline of the United Methodist Church, Stewart Memorial, through its Charge Conference, elects annually members of the Committee on Finance.

Serving on this committee are the chairperson, the pastor, lay member of the annual conference, chairperson of the Administrative Council, chairperson or representative of the Committee on Pastor-Parish Relations, a representative of the trustees elected by them, chairperson of the ministry on stewardship, lay leader, financial secretary, and treasurer.[21]

In 2006, the Committee on Finance was chaired by Collace Greene, Sr., with the following serving as members:

Franklin Boston	Andy Jackson	Samuel Sharper, Sr.
Joel Fears	Walter E. Monroe, Jr.	Carolyn Solomon[22]
Minnie Harris	Wanda Pride	
Lucy Heath	Harold Rhodes	

With the direction of the Charge Conference, the Board of Trustees, supervises, oversees, and cares for all the real property owned by the church.[23] Among the chairs of the Board of Trustees was W.R. Crooms, the first woman to hold such position.[24] She held that office for many years. In 2006, officers of the Board of Trustees were, Franklin Boston, chairperson; Willie Reed, vice chairperson and Toni Stewart, Secretary. The members were:

Class of 2006	Class of 2007	Class of 2008
Roland Blossom, Esq.	Franklin Boston	Muriel J. Bartley
Christopher Greer	Gladys Greene	Harold Rhodes
Joel Fears, Sr.	Minnie Harris	Willie Reed[25]

In 2006, the Committee on Lay Leadership was headed by the pastor, Walter E. Monroe. Other officers included Jessie

---

[21] The Book of Discipline of the United Methodist Church, 1996, 262.4.

[22] Church Officers 2006.

[23] The Book of Discipline of the United Methodist Church, 1996, 253.2.

[24] Administrative Council Minutes.

[25] Church Officers 2006, 2007, and 2008.

Childs, vice chairperson and Joel Fears, Sr., lay leader. The
members were:

Class of 2006	**Class of 2007**	**Class of 2008**
Franklin Boston	Roland Blossom	Shirley Bell
Christopher Greer	Joel Fears, Sr.	Jessie Childs
John Heath	Carolyn Solomon	S. Louise Rosemond[26]

---

[26]Idem.

Chapter 9

Its Financial Quest

While it is desirable that the church rely on tithes and offerings to finance its operation, falling short in those areas has required the church to seek other means of obtaining funds. Almost from its beginning the church has looked beyond its membership for financial support. The monetary generosity of Rev. Stewart made possible the purchase of a house for use as a sanctuary.[1] By 1900, hard-working churchgoers had found many ways to raise money. Perhaps, one of the better ways was to sponsor excursions to Jacksonville, Titusville, and other near-by places. The expansion of the Florida East Coast railroad made that possible. As early as 1901, Stewart Chapel (Stewart Memorial) was utilizing rallies to raise money for building a parsonage.[2]

Borrowing money also was a way that the church met immediate financial needs. Typical loans were the following: On May 10, 1904, the church acquired $175 from the Equitable Building and Loan Company.[3] On August 1, 1923, a ninety-day loan of $500 was acquired from the Daytona Bank and Trust Com-

---

[1]H.C. McLain and Dr. T.A. Adams "Historical Data," *The Celebration of the Forty-Fourth Anniversary of Stewart Memorial Methodist Episcopal.*

[2]*Daytona Gazette*, March 30, 1901.

[3]Contract between Trustees of Stewart Memorial Methodist Episcopal Church (Colored) and The Equitable Building and Loan Company, May, 10, 1904.

pany,[4] and on January 28, 1926, $100 were borrowed from the same bank.[5] Viewing a $175 loan from the 2006 perspective, it would be easy for a member of the congregation to say that he/she could have contributed for that amount. It brings one back to reality, however, when realizing that a loan or gift of $175 in 1904 was equivalent to $3,800 in 2006.[6] Also, contrast the forty-one-cent stamp of 2007 with the two-cent stamp of 1900.

As years passed, the location of Stewart Memorial in the heart of the African American business section of Daytona Beach enabled it to appeal successfully to business and professional people to be patrons for certain church events. Palms Market, Palms Café, Frank Brown Taylor, Clark Funeral Home, Slack Drug Store, Midway Shoe Shop, Dr. E. N. Brown (Dental Surgery) and Bethune-Cookman College—all neighboring establishments—were listed as patrons as early as 1937. This practice has long existed and continues today.[7]

The location of the church also aided it in selling items to fund its programs. Mrs. Sarah Burns, a long-time member recalled, "Many Saturdays, in front of the church, the following ladies would sell pies, fish sandwiches and home churned ice cream: Ophelia Rivers, Lucille Stephens, Ella Alums, Lillie Snell Hawkins and other faithful members."[8] While funds raised by such means might have been sufficient for that time, there came a time when there were greater needs, and different means had to be created to raise money to meet those needs.

James Huger chaired the Stewardship and Finance Committee in 1967. His committee presented a budget of $12,950 for

---

[4]Contract between Stewart Memorial M.E. Church and Daytona Bank & Trust Company, October 30, 1923.

[5]Contract between Stewart Memorial Methodist Episcopal Church and Daytona Bank and Trust Company, June 1, 1926.

[6]The Inflation Calculator, <http:www.westegg.com/inflation/infl.egi>, 5/12/2007.

[7]Stewart Memorial United Methodist Church,100th Anniversary Celebration, March 14, 1993.

[8]Idem.

the following year (Equivalent to $78,000 in 2006 according to the Inflation Calculator). Except for the $5,000, which was expected to be raised through tithes and collection, the remainder was to be raised by five rallies:

- Trustees Rally September 17

- Harvest Rally November 26

- Men's Day January 28

- Women's Day February 25

- Palm Sunday April 7[9]

In addition to the above, Loyalty Day, Family and Friends Day, Dual Day, and other special days became ways in which the church raised money. On November 26, 1973, Richard V. Moore, lay leader, warned that, "Special church rallies be a rare thing at Stewart Memorial." Our membership has been supportive. They are tired of rallies. This seems to be the growing sentiment of the membership."[10]

The 2006 budget proposed by the Finance Committee and approved by the Administrative Council and Charge Conference was based on income as follows:

Tithes	64.0%
Public Offering	04.1%
Misc. (Parsonage Rent, Donation, Interest, etc,)	06.8%
Fund Raising (Women's Day, Men's Day, other special days)	24.1%
Sunday School	00.9%[11]

Every Sunday, an opportunity is provided for the congregation to pay tithes and contribute to the church through public offering. Historically, tithes and contributions have been tied closely to the class system, which is discussed in the sub-chapter

---

[9] Administrative Board, August 27, 1967

[10] Administrative Board, November 26, 1973

[11] Information provided by Collace Greene, Chair of Finance, 1906.

on worship. Likewise, financial giving has been tied closely to stewardship. In recent history, as a prelude to the appeal for tithes and offerings the most frequently quoted scripture has been Malachi 3:10 which reads:

> Bring the full tithe into the storehouse, so that there
> may be food in my house, and thus put me to the
> test, says the Lord of hosts; see if I will not open
> the windows of heaven for you and pour down for
> you an overflowing blessing.

Regardless of the scripture used, there was always an attempt to relate giving to performance of service to honor God. Next to tithes, the greatest source of monetary funds has been that of special rallies.

During the decade of the eighties, the annual Men's and Women's Day rallies became the major fund-raising efforts of the church. In addition to seeking to obtain stated financial goals, these fund-raising observances have developed into multi-purpose occasions. They have been formed around certain themes and have been used to honor members of the church and the community. Health seminars, political forums, and other events have also preceded them.

Typical of the themes utilized for Men's Day are: Christian Men Serving God Through Discipleship (1997), Christian Men Entering The New Millennium with Faith (1998), and Christian Men: Embracing Christ in the New Millennium (2000).[12]

The occasion has been used to bring back as speakers young men who grew up in the church. Dr. Rogers P. Fair, Jr., Dr. Theodore Nicholson, Jr., Dr. David Moore, and Minister Lynn Thompson were among them. It was also used to bring back a former member who played a major part in the building of the current sanctuary—Harrison DeShields.

---

[12] All information on Men' s Day and Women's Day was obtained from souvenir programs of those occasions.

The program has been dedicated to the trustees listed on the cornerstone, military veterans, true sons of Stewart Memorial, Boys Scouts, outstanding high school students, and to Lance Corporal Nathaniel Jenkins, who was killed in the military while on duty in Lebanon. Likewise, many of the hard-working men of Stewart have been honored on these programs.

Often the men observe a week rather than a day. Typical of this was the observance of 2004, which included a health forum on the Monday night before Men's Day, in which Dr. Robert Sessom was the speaker; and on Friday night when a "Meet the Candidates" forum was held.

Women's Day has utilized such themes as: Christian Women Determined to Make A Difference (1991), Women – Diverse But Unified in Winning Souls for Christ (1995), Women: Pioneers in the Struggle for A Just and Spiritual World (2004).

They have used the occasion to honor pioneering and leading women of the area regardless of "race." They have also honored elderly members of our flock including Margaret Gibbs, who lived to observe birthdays in excess of 100 years.

The women usually scheduled a week of activities leading to the observance of Women's Day. The activities of 2004 included a Bible class, health workshop, and sacred poetry reading. During the 2005 observance, the women collected and printed a book of prayers for distribution. The special activities of the 2006 observance included a Bible class, health workshop, and sacred poetry reading.

In addition to raising needed funds and providing interesting programs, Men's Day and Women's Day afford the church an opportunity to display unity. The steering committees seek to involve all men in the preparation of successful Men's Day programs and the same is done in the case of women in the Women's Day program. On the financial side, the entire church membership is involved in each of the endeavors.

While rallies have been used to secure funds for programs of Stewart Memorial, tithes remain the basic source of income for the church. The giving of tithes is encouraged each Sunday by Scriptural references. As good stewards, we are expected to give to support the church and its mission, preferably through tithing. Because money is essential for carrying on the operation of the church, the Finance Committee has a major task. Giving financially is a meaningful way in which we can express gratitude to God for the many blessings He has bestowed upon us.

Chapter 10

Stewardship

Stewardship has always been an important part of the life of Stewart Memorial. While it has not been possible to identify the earliest stewards, we can list those who held office in 1947. They were:

J.H. Anglin	Mai Crawford	Shelly Smith
H.E. Bartley	Thomas Graham	Cleo Trapp
L.R. Brassell	Alphonso Jones	E.P. Trapp[1]
E.N. Brown	J.L. Slack	
D.C. Colbert	Joseph Smith	

The Stewardship and Finance Committee, which later became the Stewardship Committee, has almost always utilized teams to achieve its financial purposes. In 1962, a Stewardship Emphasis was organized, and its team captains were:

Anthony Stephens	Florence Small	William Davis
Charles Cherry	Hariette Davis	John Heath
Eloise Williams	Margaret Bartley	W.R. Crooms
Lottie DeBose	Selina Clemons	Olivia Jones
Flossie Curington	Henry Anglin	Rogers P. Fair

---

[1] Handbook of Stewart Memorial Methodist Church, 1893–1947.

Margaret Gibbs   C.S. Shears
Virginia Fulword   Frank Brown
Agnes Fair   Richard Bell[2]

In 1967, there existed a commission on Stewardship and Finance, headed by James Huger. By 1973, however, Stewardship had become a separate entity, chaired by William Kornegay who simultaneously was chairman of Finance. During his tenure as chairman of Stewardship, he sought to promote its enhancement. In order to increase awareness of the congregation of the importance of stewardship, seminars and workshops were conducted, including the seminar of January 16, 1973, which Kornegay coordinated. The film, "The Questors" was shown and was followed by a discussion led by J. Griffen Greene. The seminar was sponsored by Theodore Jones, chairperson of the Council on Ministry and Harry L. Burney, chairperson of the special committee.[3] On July 8, 1973 Stewardship was the theme of the Key 73 seminar for that date, under the leadership of Florence Roane. Kornegay assisted with the discussion.[4]

Pamphlets also were distributed to promote stewardship, including "Stewardship and You," which perceives a Christian steward as one who "serves God out of love and gratitude for these gifts (health, time, talent, property, the Gospel, etc.), knowing that it's **not** how much we have but what we **do** with **what we have** that is important."[5] Also utilized was a brochure entitled "Stewardship," which was prepared by Eleanor Hurry, co-chair of the Work Area on Stewardship of the Deland District. According to that document, one can be described as having the qualities of a good steward if he/she gives: "time, prayers, skills, and money willingly and joyfully—and in proportion to what one has received."[6]

---

[2]*Stewart Memorial Herald*, 1962, 1.
[3]Special Handout.
[4]Church Bulletin, July 8, 1973.
[5]Channing L. Bete, *Stewardship and You* (South Deerfield MA, 1996), 3.
[6]Eleanor E. Hurry, M.D., Ed. D., of the Deland District Stewardship Work

A close relationship existed between class leaders and stewardship. On April 10, 1984, a class leaders Workshop and Stewardship meeting was held. Attending this two-hour workshop were class leaders and members of their respective classes. The call for this meeting read: "We will look at the program and the budget of the church, and assess our responsibility for meeting the challenge." Consultants for this workshop were the pastor, Rogers P. Fair; Lay Leader, Richard V. Moore; Chairperson of Finance, George Whitehead; Chairperson on Council of Ministry, Phannye B. Huger; Administrative Board Chairperson, Bernard Irvin; and Business Manager, James E. Huger.[7]

Rev. Carrill Munnings took an active role in seeking to promote the goals of "Stewardship Month." He wrote:

> I believe that we can attain good stewardship this
> month ... if we try! Let us focus on our covenant
> relationship with and what it means to us in relation
> to our stewardship of time, talent and treasure. Let
> us seize the opportunity, now in the present, to be
> the faithful stewards that God is calling us to be.
> Let us trust God at his word for the increase in our
> stewardship; and let us be faithful to Him, obeying
> all of his commandments and receiving all of his
> blessings. Truly, we are servants of Christ in that
> we, the church, do not exist to glorify ourselves,
> but to glorify and give attention to Christ. And, we
> are stewards of the mysteries of god if we abide in
> God's mysteries trusting that "if we give... it shall
> be given to us" pressed down, shaken together and
> running over." (Luke 6:38.)[8]

By May 29, 1994, the Stewardship Committee was hosted by Minnie Harris. Among the activities she used to promote

---

Area, "Stewardship," n.d..

[7] Church Bulletin, March 25, 1984.

[8] *SMUMC News*, March 1993, Vol 3, No. 3.

stewardship was a Dinner Celebration for the membership of Stewart Memorial. In hosting this activity, she made these challenging remarks:

> We are here today to celebrate all members who responded to God as good and faithful stewards. This is a Stewardship "Thank You" Dinner. The Stewardship Committee agrees that each of you deserves a "pat on the back" for growth in your relationship with God through prayer, presence in worship, giving and serving. When we define stewardship as a way to get people to give money, we skew the biblical story and send people away. But when a church begins from a stewardship perspective, as Stewart Memorial does, the local congregation moves from a fund raising and funding ministry focus.

In making a distinction between fund raising and funding ministry, Mrs. Harris defined fund raising as raising money "regardless of what it does to the steward" and funding ministry as helping "the steward in the journey of receiving and giving and is centered around the steward's response to the good news of Jesus Christ." She continued:

> When we move the focus from fund raising to funding ministry, we change the message from "Give to the church because it needs it" to "Give through the church to participate in and accomplish God's purpose in the world as we know it in Jesus Christ." Because Stewardship is the most visible of the faith discipline, we tell the "Stewardship Story" in our daily words and actions—our story is one of faithfulness.[9]

---

[9] *SMUMC News*, 9 Jan 1994, Vol. 4, No.6.

Many different persons and organizations contributed to the dinner.

After a successful 1994 Stewardship Dinner, Mrs. Harris announced the observance of the 2nd Annual Stewardship and Commitment Sunday for the second Sunday in August 1995. The theme of the morning services for that day was **commitment**. It was followed by a stewardship luncheon.[10]

Persons becoming members of the Methodist Church agree to uphold it with their prayers, presence, gifts and services. According to the booklet, *Stewardship and You*, "Each of us can share in God's plan in his or her own way." Attention is given to the several ways one can use his/her talent in the chapter of Worship. In addition to those, there are others means of using one's talent. Firstly, in the case of employed persons, they are to be credited with their sincere efforts. Through the years, several persons have provided secretarial services for the church, including: Gladys Greene, Margaret Watson, Jennifer Snow and Jessie Childs. They used their talents, effectively, and earned the praise of the church. Keeping the sanctuary and grounds beautifully can be attributed to such persons as Albert Edwards, Jr., Calvin Tynes, Franklin and Annie Boston. In cases where they were paid, partially, for their services, they often went beyond the call of duty.

Others also employed their God-given talents to serve God. Numerous were those whose professional careers were in teaching, who employed those skills in teaching church school and vacation Bible School. Lawrence Temple, Sr., a former art instructor, uses his talent in any way the church desires it. Maxine Temple, his wife delighted the congregation with her many saxophone solos. Attention has been given to the talented choirs elsewhere, but on occasions where they have not been available for performances, Virginia Brigety Fulword and Toni Stewart have displayed their musical talents. The special piano concert by Gladys Greene and recital by Shirley Watts Bing are dis-

---

[10]Administrative Board, July 10, 1995.

cussed elsewhere.

Numerous programs have been made memorable by the poetry-reciting of Mary Alice Smith, Cleo Higgins, B. J. Moore, and Thurman Standback. In May 2005, Higgins joined with Willie Bolden in a poetry recital. Mary Fears also has used her talent in story-telling to enlighten the congregation. Shirley Watts Bing and Jake C. Miller have been gifted in poetry-writing, and their printed works have appeared on souvenir programs for Men's Day, Women's Day, special occasions, funeral programs and church bulletins.

The landscaping talent of Willie Reed was used to beautify the grounds of Stewart Memorial, and the technical skills of Joel Fears, Sr. have been utilized in so many ways. Those, who possess cooking skills, have provided tasty meals and snacks for the congregation and visiting groups.

The talents shown by those listed above and elsewhere in this manuscript, are indicative of effective stewardship in time and talent, as well as financial gifts. This type of stewardship has made Stewart Memorial a more effective church. Because of the importance of stewardship, it is essential that it be emphasized in pastoral sermons, Church School classes, printed material, and through other means.

Chapter 11

Its Ministries

According to the *Book of Discipline*, "Each local congregation shall provide a comprehensive program of nurture, outreach, and witness..."[1] For several decades, these programs were branches of the Council on Ministries, which at various times were chaired by Theodore T. Jones, Theodore Nicholson, Phannye Huger, and Shelia Jackson.[2]

In 1996, the Administrative Board, chaired by Sallie Shelton Culver, was renamed the Administrative Council. According to the reorganization plan the Council on Ministry was replaced with five ministries: Outreach, Nurture and Caring, Worship, Growth and Enrichment, and Events.[3] Utilizing these five ministries, we will look at the various programs of the church. An activity discussed under one of these topics does not necessarily mean that a particular ministry is performing it.

The duties set out for the **Outreach Ministry** were "to plan and implement programs" designed to meet the needs and respond to the concerns of persons beyond the congregation. It seeks to relate the ministry of the church to the needs of the wider community. The following activities were placed

---

[1] BD The Book of Discipline of the United Methodist Church, 1996.
[2] Administrative Board meetings.
[3] Administrative Board *Action News*, July 15, 1996.

under the jurisdiction of this ministry: evangelism, mission, church and society, religion and "race," Christian unity and inter-religious concerns, disaster relief, status and role of women, scouting, and membership secretary.[4]

The Purpose assigned to the **Nurture and Caring Ministry** was "to plan and implement programs related to the spiritual growth and special needs of the membership and others for 'building the body of Christ'" (Eph. 4:12). Health and welfare, adults, young adults, youth, children, scholarship, grief ministry and class leaders were the concern of this ministry.[5]

The **Worship Ministry** was given the duty of planning and providing opportunities for giving thanks and praise, for dedicating lives to Christian discipleships and for celebrating the events of the Christian faith in an attitude of reverence. Among this ministry's concerns are activities involving: music, ushers, stewards, acolytes, lay speakers, lay ministers, greeters and special services (Laity Sunday, Stewardship, Revival, Ash Wednesday, etc.)[6]

The **Growth and Enrichment Ministry** seeks to offer programs that would strengthen one for ministry to others, in order for all to grow in the Christian faith and become disciples. It is responsible for education, Church School, Vacation Bible School, resources, Disciple Bible Study, Bible Study, retreats and long-range planning.[7]

The **Events Ministry**'s main task is "to plan and implement fellowship activities for the membership and others." Banquets, picnics, birthday breakfast and special days are activities for which the Events Ministry is responsible.[8]

After this reorganization plan was approved, the initial heads of these ministries were:

---

[4]Program Calendar and Membership Directory, 1998, 2-3.
[5]Ibid.
[6]Ibid.
[7]Ibid.
[8]Ibid.

- Outreach: Juanita Sharper, chair; B. J, Moore, co-chair

- Growth and Enrichment: Jake C. Miller

- Worship: Shirley Watts-Bing

- Nurture & Caring: Minnie J. Harris, chair; Jean McLean, co-chair

- Events: Jessie Childs and Shelia Jackson, co-chairs[9]

As indicated earlier, the five ministries include sub-ministries. In 2006 specialized ministries were chaired by the following:

- Christian Unity and Inter-religious Concerns: Bobbie Sweeting

- Church and Society: Vivian N. Davis

- Health and Welfare: Annie Bell, Mabel Saxon, Mary Slater

- Disaster Response: Harold Heard

- Community Volunteers: Jessie Childs

- Education: Celestine Hinson

- Higher Education and Campus Ministry: Mary Alice Smith

- Missions: Muriel J. Bartley, Mary Fears

- Religion and "Race": Senorita Locklear

- Status and Role of Women: Paulette Monroe

- Stewardship: Minnie Harris

- Worship: S. Louise Rosemond

---

[9]Ibid., 6.

- Children's Home Representative: Vera Barragan

- Evangelism: Vanessa Frazier

- Superintendent of Church School: Minister Willie Scott

- Prayer Advocacy: Juanita Sharper

- Coordinator of Children's Ministries: Janette Gibson

- Coordinator of Youth Ministries: Wanda Pride[10]

Projected for the 2007-year was a revised ministry format, which altered the old ministries as follow:

Nurture and Care Umbrella – consisting of the Children, Youth, Adult/Family, Persons with Disabilities, Disaster Response, Health and Welfare, Parish Nurse, Prayer, Stewardship and Worship Ministries.

Outreach Umbrella – consisting of Children's Home, Community Volunteers, Higher Education and Campus Ministry, Missions, Religion and "Race," Scouting, Status and Role of Women, Canned Goods Program – Halifax Urban Ministries.

Witness Umbrella – which embraces the Evangelism Ministry.[11]

---

[10]*SMUMC*, Church Officers, 2006.

[11]*SMUMC*, Welcome to Our Church Brochure, 2007.

Chapter 12

Worship Ministry

> Each can worship God in a way that is special,
> Since each possesses a talent that is very rare.
> When in our churches we demonstrate our talents,
> We show praises to God for His loving care.

Persons who attend church can participate in worship in a variety of ways. Ministers deliver sermons, lay persons preside over the services, musicians provide music, ushers facilitate the comfort of the people, and congregations participate throughout the services. In the Worship Resource Guide, the purpose of the Worship Committee is:

> to assist members of the Family of God in expe-
> riencing a warm meaningful communion with our
> Creator, Provider, Protector and Friend. To lend
> energy and suggestions to foster a meaningful, or-
> derly flowing worship service. To give assistance
> to the pastor and all phases of worship, so as to as-
> sure spirit-filled orderly worship services with min-
> imum distractions. Response should be to the ONE
> being worshiped not to the one leading or partici-
> pating in worship.[1]

---

[1]Bing, Shirley W. (Worship Chair)"Worship Resource Guide," *SMUMC*

Discussed below are some of the leading components of the Worship Ministry.

Music Ministry

Historically, music has been an essential part of worship. The *Book of Psalms* was written for praise and musical purposes. At Stewart Memorial, psalms continue to be used for those purposes. While there is no one alive who can give eye account of the first services at the initial church, we are certain that Thomas Walker utilized a lot of singing in these opening services. As the church grew, major musical responsibilities, probably, shifted from the congregation to the choir. The lack of records makes it impossible for us to describe the earliest music ministry, but as the church progressed, some of the musicians could be identified. Historical accounts indicate that Virginia Darby (Fulword), one of the church's noted vocalists until the late 1990s, was performing solos at Stewart Memorial as early as 1937.[2] The 1947 Handbook praised the work of Anthony Stephens as president of the Senior Choir. The work of Olivia Jones as organist for the Senior Choir and that of Willie Mobley and Wynona Brown of the Junior Choir also were recognized.[3]

Through the years, the Music Ministry has undergone many changes. At the time of the dedication of the new church edifice in 1973, the church organists were: Shirley Watts (Bing), Mary Poole (Cook), and Herbert Harris, Sr. The directors of choirs were as follow: B. J. Moore, (Adult), Harry L. Burney, Jr. (Male) and Mary Poole (Gospel).[4]

In 1993, when Stewart Memorial celebrated its 100th anniversary, the Music Ministry had several choirs, including the

---

1998-1999, Compiled by the Worship Committee, p. 2.

[2]The Celebration of the Forty-Fourth Anniversary of Stewart Memorial Methodist Episcopal Church, Souvenir Program, December 15-19, 1937.

[3]Handbook of Stewart Memorial Methodist Church, 1893 –1947.

[4]Consecration Celebration: A Service of Consecration and Open House, Stewart Memorial United Methodist Church, April 15, 1973.

Chancel Choir, (under the direction of Toni Stewart) Volunteer Choir (Herbert Harris), and Children Choir (Olive Lewis).

Stewart Memorial was blessed with a number of musicians who provided music for worship services, including: Olive Lewis and Herbert Harris (organists); and Maxine Temple, Eloise Williams and Toni Stewart (pianists).[5]

In August 1998, the Program and Ministries Committee recommended "immediate employment of music staff to revolutionize the music aspect of the worship service in order to energize the membership and congregation."[6] A minister of music was hired following the approval of the recommendation by the Administrative Council. Charles Jackson became the first minister and Toni Stewart followed him. In 2006, the Music Ministry was headed by Charles Long until his illness, when he was replaced by Kevin Cooper. According to the Worship Guide, a major duty of the minister of music is to "coordinate and communicate with the pastor and Worship Chair/Committee regarding the music and choir participation in worship services and other special events of the church."[7] In this ministry there are four regular choirs: the Chancel Choir, Male Choir, Youth/Children Choir, and Voices of Joy Gospel Choir, with each performing one Sunday per month. The Volunteer Choir sings on special occasions and on the fifth Sunday.[8]

In addition to its regular assignments, the Music Ministry has performed many useful roles at the church. Musical concerts have been a historical practice at Stewart Memorial. "Music Through the Years," presented on December 9, 1973, was one of such concerts. These periodic musical programs were taken to another level in 1980 when Lucien Lewis and Olive Lewis introduced the annual Christmas cantata. This extraordi-

---

[5]*Celebration*, March 14, 1993.

[6]*SMUMC*, Program and Ministries Committee Recommendations of the Long Range Planning Committee, August 17, 1998.

[7]*Worship Resource Guide*.

[8]Church Bulletins.

nary musical recital utilized the talents of members of Stewart
Memorial, as well as those of other churches.[9] Mr. Lewis's
death some time later was a tragic loss to Stewart Memorial and
the world of music. Determined to carry out the Christmas tradition, Dr. Eddie J. Rivers, pastor, substituted a candle light vigil
for the cantata in 1986.[10] After a brief interlude, the traditional
program was returned with Charlie Long as director and Olive
Lewis as organist.

In 1992, the Christmas choirs of Stewart Memorial and
Allen Chapel A.M.E. Church joined to present two Christmas
concerts. Charlie Long and Barbara Bouie served as joint
directors. As with the early cantatas, participants from other
churches in the community displayed their talent. A concert
was presented at each of the two sponsoring churches.[11] The
joint sponsorship of the Christmas cantata continued for several
years. In 1997, the two churches presented a musical drama,
entitled "Hallelujah, Jesus the Savior is Born." The presentation
was written and directed by Audre Chantel Davis.[12]

As Minister of Music, Toni Stewart also presented Christmas recitals, including the one of December 24, 2000 entitled:
"Twas This Christmas Celebration." Presented during the regular church services, the program utilized all choirs, soloists,
other musicians, and narrators. Willie Frank Bolden was the
organist for the occasion.

In addition to Christmas cantatas, several other interesting
programs have been presented by the Music Ministry or by persons associated with it, including concerts by Shirley W. Bing,
and Gladys Greene. Bing, whose contributions in the Youth
Ministry, Worship Ministry and Music Ministry have been applauded, presented "A Living Memorial Musical Tribute" on
August 9, 1992. The recital was given to honor persons who

---

[9]*SMUMC*, The Fourth Annual Christmas Concert, December 18, 1983
(Souvenir Program).

[10]Burns, Sarah, "Historical Reflections," *Celebration*, March 14, 1993.

[11]*SMUMC News*, November 1992.

[12]*The Vine*, December 1997.

had made worthy contributions to humanity. Bing's repertoire included a variety of music. The mezzo-soprano was accompanied by Barbara McNeely Bouie. The concert, presented before a standing room audience, was followed by the dedication of five elm trees as "living memorials to the fifty-two honorees." Bing received voice lessons from Gail Robinson Oturu of Bethune-Cookman College.[13]

The Music Ministry also presented Gladys M. Greene in a "recital of praise and thanksgiving" on September 28, 1997. The title of the recital, "His Love to Me, I Give to You," expressed Greene's thankfulness to God for having been able to serve Him through service to her church. In her introductory statement in the souvenir booklet, she wrote:

> Thank you for sharing this witness experience with me. It is born of a new awakening of my spiritual essence due to responding to the opportunities to serve my church as a member, Class Leader, a student of the Bible, a Lay Speaker and a grateful recipient of God's bountiful and abiding grace.

Her repertoire included hymns of praise, faith, guidance and witnessing. It also included music from such composers as Handel and Beethoven. Greene's serious study of piano began on a part-time basis during the Fall of 1979 and continued through the Summer of 1984. The recital was performed before an enthusiastic audience.[14]

A musical program devoted to the singing of African-American songs, organized by Mary Fears, was another memorable musical program at Stewart Memorial. Held as a part of the annual Women's Day activity, the program drew people from throughout the county, and as far away as

---

[13] A Living Memorial Musical Tribute (August 9, 1992) and ("A Living Memorial" *SMUMC News* Vol. 2, No. 9, September 1992).

[14] The Area of Music Ministry Presents Mrs. Gladys M/ Greene, Sunday, September 28, 1997 (program).

Jacksonville. Fears remarked: "What I'm trying to do is get people to be aware of the contributions of African Americans in the history of America." She viewed the "mournful, prayerful, rousing music slaves left as a legacy" that should be "embraced with pride." This program, which was not presented by the music ministry, but through the organized efforts of Fears, won applause from the press and those who attended. Araminta Lake observed: "The ingenuity and pride and all of those things that make us what we are as Americans and African American, those stories have to be told." Lake, one of the lead singers, is a middle school mathematics teacher from Deland.[15]

In October 2006, Frank Boston orchestrated a pre-Men's Day musical program, entitled "Singing in the Old Time Way."[16] Later in the year, the children of Stewart Memorial, under the leadership of Rose Greene Wilson, presented a Christmas concert. Special thanks were given to Angie Polite, Janette Gibson, Sharon Workman, and all who made the December 24th concert a success.[17]

Through the years, many other musical programs have been presented, including the Afternoon of Music sponsored by the youth of Stewart on April 29, 1984, which featured youth choirs from several churches. That program, however, is discussed in the chapter on youth activities.

Lay Speakers

Although one may not have the talent to sing, or one may not have the calling to preach, an individual can worship God in numerous ways. One way is to serve as a lay speaker.

Lay speakers perform many functions for the local church. They assist the pastor in the conduct of religious services and activities, and they may be called upon to give sermons or ad-

---

[15]"Memories of Song and Spirit," *Daytona Beach News-Journal*, April 10, 2005.

[16]Handout.

[17]Church Bulletin, December 17, 2006.

dresses. According to the *Book of Discipline*, the lay speaker is one:

> who is well informed on the Scriptures and the doc-
> trine, heritage, organization, and life of the United
> Methodist Church and who has received specific
> training to develop skills in witnessing to the Chris-
> tian faith through spoken communication, church
> and community leadership, and care-giving min-
> istries.[18]

In the performance of their duties, the Worship Ministry suggests that lay speakers possess pleasant voices and "put forth every effort to be an asset to the service, to be heard by all worshipers, and follow the bulletin as outlined (in order) without announcing each and every item singularly."[19]

In 1972, under the pastorate of Rogers P. Fair, the lay speakers were organized. Included were: Richard V. Moore, Harry Burney, Jr., Mary Morse, Joel Fears, Sr., Harrison DeShields and George Whitehead.[20] A year later, Theodore Jones, James Huger, Florence Roane and Theodore Nicholson joined them.[21] By 1976 the certified lay speakers had a more coordinated program. Theodore Nicholson was the coordinator. The certified speakers included:

James Huger   Harry L. Burney, Jr.
Richard V. Moore   Florence L. Roane
George Whitehead   Harrison DeShields
Theodore T. Jones   Joel Fears (On Leave)[22]
Mary Morse

---

[18]*Book of Discipline*, 270.
[19]Worship Resource Guide.
[20]Memorandum from Mrs. Agnes Fair, June18, 2006.
[21]*Consecration*, April 15, 1973.
[22]Church Bulletin, April 11, 1976.

For 2007, lay speakers are listed in two categories—certified lay speakers and local lay speakers. Those two groups include:

Local

Bernard Irvin   Andy Jackson, Sr.
Franklin Boston   B.J. Moore
Bernard Irvin

Certified

Sallie Shelton Culver   Collace Greene, Sr.
Paulette Monroe   Theodore Nicholson
Joel V. Fears, Sr.   John Heath
Merceda G. Nicholson   Mary Alice Smith[23]
Andy Jackson, Sr.

Ushers

According to the *Worship Resource Guide*, ushers are "to serve the church by providing directions and assistance to worshippers, thus sharing the responsibility of creating the atmosphere for a smoothly moving worship experience."[24] The 1947 Handbook gave this description of the usher ministry.

> This fine group of well-trained ushers is anxious that every worshipper who comes to Stewart Memorial will have comfort during the services. They greet you at the door with the Order of Worship and a hymnal and, conducting you to your pew, one is enhanced by the friendly atmosphere. E. P. Trapp, president of the Board of Ushers, is familiar to many people who have worshipped at Stewart Memorial for he is ever awake to every

[23] *Directory*, 2007.
[24] *Worship Resource Guide*.

need of the worshiper.   The board meets each
Thursday evening at eight o'clock.[25]

For more than forty-five years, Eloise Edwards-Snell served
faithfully as president of the Ushers Board. During that time
many banquets and other social functions were held. Likewise,
annual programs were presented at Stewart Memorial, usually
on the third Sunday in April as a part of the monthly activities of
the City-Wide Ushers Union, which rotates among its member
churches. The money raised on that occasion remains at the
sponsoring church. Snell served as president of the City-Wide
Ushers for eight years.[26]

Under the Snell administration, annual gifts were given to
the church, mostly through Men's and Women's Day activities. It also contributed to the church such items as the outside
bulletin board, word processor, hymnals, chairs, kitchen supplies and other monetary gifts.[27] For its outstanding service, the
Usher Board was honored at the June 2, 1991 Pastor's Breakfast,
and Snell was honored at the 2006 Women's Day program.[28]

The Usher Board is organized into senior and junior ushers,
with the junior ushers serving every third Sunday. In 2006,
the Usher Board Ministry was headed by Delores Davis.
Ushers included: Senorita Locklear, Eloise Edwards-Snell,
Annie Boston, Gloria Fordham, Johnny Pride, Johnnie A.
Stewart, Sharon Workman, Elaine Sharper-Brown, Joseph
Brown, Harold Heard, and Willie Ware. Junior ushers included
Christopher Jackson, D'John Greer, Christopher Greer and
Phillip Conage.[29]

---

[25]Handbook, 8.

[26]Memorandum from Mrs. Eloise Snell.

[27]Memorandum, and Observations as an Usher.

[28]*SMUMC News*, June 1991.

[29]*SMUMC*, Annual Men's Day Celebration, 2006.

Hospitality Greeters

The ministry task assigned the Hospitality Greeters is "to greet and register visitors, make announcements, initiate fellowship period within the worship service, and serve as host and hostess at various church functions where appropriate and available." Initially, the members were: Clarence N. Childs, Jessie J. Childs, Alberta Greene, Minnie Harris, Celestine Hinson, David Hinson (Deceased), Linda Huger, Sophia Huger, Thelma Irvin, Dedra Jackson, Christopher Jackson, Shelia Jackson, Carrie Lee, Kendra Newman, Wanda Pride, Johna Pride, Samuel Sharper, Sr., Anya Solomon, Carolyn Solomon, and Dr. Ralph Solomon.[30] These hospitality greeters, through their efforts, extend welcome to newcomers to the church.

Acolytes

According to the Worship Resource Guide, the Acolytes "are to assist the Pastor, Ushers, and Communion Stewards in such tasks as the following: lighting, extinguishing the candles, carrying the light out, assisting with offering when needed and assisting with Communion and Baptism."[31]

The acolytes were organized in 1972 under the pastoral charge of Rogers P. Fair, with Shirley Moore as sponsor. On January 13, 1973, the first of four training sessions were held for the acolytes. Ten young men were sought to begin this vital program.[32] A party was given on August 24, 1973, to recognize the acolytes. Shirley Moore, sponsor, and Stephen Jenkins, president, headed the committee to make the preparations. Also participating on this committee were Thelma Irvin, Juanita Sharper, Dorothy Kornegay, Jessie Childs and Neo Garvin.[33]

During the pastoral charge of Carrill Munnings, the acolytes

---

[30]Interview with Jessie J. Childs.
[31]Worship Resource Guide.
[32]Church Bulletin, January 7, 1973.
[33]*SMUMC News*, August 1972.

were reorganized, with Nathalie C. Jenkins playing a major role in this effort. Under her leadership the 2001 acolytes were Christopher Greer, Marie Huger, Christopher Jackson, Dedra Jackson, Johna Pride, Virginia Smith, and Anya Solomon.[34]

In 2006, Janette Gibson served as coordinator of the program. The members were Cherell, Jonathan, and Sherlyn Davis, Erik Greer, Candace Harris, Jordan Pride and Jamal, Jamaree, and Jamoya Hughes.[35]

Acolytes are reminded that, "Assisting in the worship service is an honor and should be treated as such." According to the Worship Guide Book: serving as acolytes gives the youngsters the opportunity to learn quite a great deal about the church through study and active duty in performing these important and significant religious responsibilities.[36]

Communion Stewards

The office of communion steward probably dates back to the first year of the church, since the ritual of the Lord's Supper is a paramount feature of the Methodist Church. Their duties are defined as: "to serve by assisting ministerial staff with communion for shut-ins, caring for and securing Communion and Baptismal cloths, Communion ware and elements. Preparing altar for Communion and Baptismal Services."[37]

The Communion Stewards in 1972 were:

Rosa Lucas, President	Dorothy Hogan
Juanita Sharper	Margaret Gibbs
Nathalie Jenkins	Hattie Willis
Willie M. Doelger	Luvenia Dukes[38]

---

[34] *Directory.*
[35] Ibid.
[36] Worship Resource Guide.
[37] Ibid.
[38] Church Bulletin, September 3, 1972.

Of those who were communion stewards in 1972, the only one still serving in 2006 was Juanita Sharper. Newer members have joined this group of Christian servants. Those serving as Communion stewards in 2006 were:

Gladys Greene   Gracie Gude
Juanita Sharper   Eloise Edwards Snell
Herlene Wilkerson   Annie Boston[39]

Eloise Snell recalls that she joined the Communion Stewards after being approached by Rosa Lucas about serving. She remembered telling her that she could not give an immediate answer, but had to pray about it. After prayerful consideration, she agreed to serve, and has been on the Board for more than twenty-five years.[40]   Others could relate similar experiences, since consenting to serve as a Communion Steward requires prayerful consideration.

Following the First Sunday Communion at the church, communion stewards faithfully accompany the pastor to pray for and commune the ill and shut-in.

Ministerial Support

The church has been enriched by the number of ministerial students and retired ministers who worship at Stewart Memorial. Even when Rogers Fair and Eddie Rivers held other positions in the area, they were regular participants in the religious services at the church. The same is true with Golden Smith, who, after his retirement, worships on a regular basis. Oswald P. Bronson, also, is a regular participant, and was when he was president of Bethune-Cookman College. Likewise, Minister George Whitehead of St. Joseph UMC in Deland, FL and Minister Willie Scott of St. Stephens in Hastings, FL, attend and participate in

---

[39]Observations.
[40]Memorandum from Mrs. Eloise Snell.

services at Stewart Memorial when they are not required to be at their churches.

Among others who performed useful services at Stewart Memorial prior to their move to higher positions were David Allen, who in 2006 was pastor of Hope of Glory in St. Petersburg, FL; Kevin James, former Superintendent of the St. Petersburg District, and the 2006 pastor of Palma Ceia UMC in Tampa; and the late Bobby Bradley, who in 2006 was serving as pastor of Mount Pleasant in Gainesville. Many other ministers have served in supporting roles at Stewart Memorial.[41]

Various pastors have sought to encourage those going into the ministry. Six individuals—three men and three women—were encouraged as they explored their calls to the ministry during the two-year tenure of Joreatha Capers. Carrill Munnings, as pastor, led and taught a pre-seminarian Discipleship group. Other pastors also have sought to be helpful.

Not only is the Worship Committee concerned with the participants in worship services, but the occasions, themselves. Christmas, Easter, and many other events are observed including: Thanksgiving, Day of Pentecost, Laity Sunday, Human Relations Day, One Great Hour of Sharing, World Communion Sunday, United Methodist Student Day, Peace with Justice Sunday, and Native American Awareness Sunday. Most of the above are designated as special days by the United Methodist Church.[42] The two which have received the most attention have been Laity Day and the United Methodist Student Day.

Celebrating Christmas

In its November 1971 meeting, the Council on Ministries proposed a worship in the Home during the Christmas season.[43] Shirley W. Bing was credited with developing the format for this unique program. Christmas in the Home has become an annual

---

[41]Review of Church Bulletins and Author's recollections..

[42]*Book of Discipline*, 267.

[43]Church Bulletin, November 1, 1971.

tradition at Stewart Memorial. Usually several families agree to host this event, but when difficulties prevented this from being done, the event was held in the Fellowship Hall of the church.

At Stewart Memorial, the Christmas season is usually one of many activities. A typical season of celebration was that of 1996. Shelia Jackson, chair of the Council on Ministries applauded the following:

> Jean McLean, Dorothy Perkins and their committee for "distributing love baskets to our sick and shut in and to persons in the community who were in need."

> Michelle Thompson for organizing the "Pick an Angel" Christmas Gift Tree. Her project to help those in need was credited with "reminding us to celebrate and give to those less fortunate."

> Shirley Bing for arranging the ritual used for the "Christmas in the Home," which has been in existence since 1971.

> Olive Lewis and Charlie Long were applauded for a wonderful performance of the Christmas cantata that was a joint presentation of Stewart Memorial and Allen Chapel A.M.E. Church. All performers were congratulated. The Christmas cantata had been an annual affair since 1981.

> Linda Huger was thanked for her "hard work and dedication to our children and youth of our church." The Christmas program presented on December 15 was widely applauded.

> Appreciation was expressed to Mary Fears for her "Book Exchange" held in the parking lot of the church. This event permitted parents and children to purchase and receive books about African Amer-

icans.[44]

Pastors have played meaningful roles in creating the Christmas spirit at the church. Rev. and Mrs. Alfonso Delaney composed "A Christmas Prayer," which reads:

> Almighty God, who resides in heaven among the twinkling stars during this Christmas season help us to focus our individual attention upon thee.
>
> Open our minds and cast out all of those ungodly thoughts. After the cleansing, fill our minds with knowledge, understanding and wisdom through the power of thy Word.
>
> Open our hearts and dissolve the growing callouses. Cleanse our hearts with the detergent that will remove stains of hatred, jealousy, envy, resentment, prejudice and malice. After the cleansing Lord, fill the heart with thy unconditional love.
>
> Open our souls and allow it to soak in the blood of our Savior. Afterwards, fill it with the gift of salvation.
>
> Open our eyes and remove the specks that prevent us from seeing the light of Christ Jesus.
>
> May we celebrate the birth of Jesus with joy, happiness and peace throughout the universe during this Christmas season, is my prayer. In the name of the Father, the Son and the Holy Spirit.
>
> Amen, Amen, Amen.[45]

Kevin James posed this challenge in an article written for the church:

---

[44]Council on Ministries Report, 1996.
[45]Handout.

Allow me to remind you that Christmas is not the
following: Kissing under the mistletoe; sipping
eggnog and attending secular parties, seeing how
many gifts can be purchased or received; and
Christmas is certainly not Santa Claus coming
from the North Pole. Christmas is Jesus' coming
to save our souls. The word Christmas is two
syllables - Christ plus Mass (coming together) and
means a mass celebration in commemoration of
the birth of Jesus Christ, the Savior of the World.
Christmas is another opportunity to encounter the
Savior as the gift of salvation. It is living and
sharing the good news of the Bethlehem story and
experiencing Jesus as the reason for the season.[46]

Observing Easter

Traditionally Easter has been a joyful occasion at Stewart
Memorial. Many remember the Easter programs given by children and the Easter Egg Hunts. Through the years the programs
have continued to exist, but in different forms. Unique was the
Easter celebration of 2006, in which Walter E. Monroe, pastor,
led the Congregation in celebrating the new birth that took
place following the resurrection of Christ with the confirmation
of twelve new members of Stewart Memorial. Those confirmed
were: Kern Cox (Adult), Jonathan Davis, David Ellis (Adult),
Erik Greer, Eric Polite, Marcus Ray, Michael Ray, Julian Smith,
Brianna Thompson, Lenore Thompson, Stephanie Thompson,
and Rashad Williams.[47]

Among the variety of Easter activities which have charac-
terized this sacred observance at Stewart Memorial are:

- Easter Sunrise Services on the beach, at the Ocean Center,
  and at various churches.

---

[46] *The Vine* Vol. 2, December 1997.
[47] Information from Mrs. Jessie Childs.

- Easter pageants as the one sponsored by the Young Active Christians of Stewart,

- Passion and Resurrection, directed by Joyce Elliott.

- Easter in the Home (A program similar to Christmas in the Home).

- Presentation of the Seven Last Words.[48]

Laity Sunday

Laity Sunday calls the church to celebrate the ministry of all lay Christians, as their lives are empowered for ministry by the Holy Spirit.[49] Through the years, this Sunday has been observed, but for most of its early history, it was known as Laymen's Day. At Stewart Memorial, this annual event has been observed in a variety of ways and it has included speakers from the church and the community.

Typical of out-of-town speakers was Dr. T. Winston Cole, an administrator of the University of Florida, who was speaker for Laymen Day, 1971.[50] Speakers from the church included James E. Huger in 1986 and Theodore Nicholson, Sr. in 1992.[51] Stewart Memorial also has made use of female talent in the presentation of Laity Day services. Mary Alice Smith was the speaker in 1997.[52] A different format was used in 1993, when the theme was "Rejoice! God's People Sing with Joy." As implied by the theme, the program was devoted to an hour of worship through the singing of hymns.[53] The 2006 Laity Day was unique inasmuch as the three speakers were young adults, who

---

[48] Observations.

[49] *Book of Discipline*, 268.2.

[50] Church Bulletin, October 10, 1971.

[51] *SMUMC News*, October 1986 and October 1992.

[52] *The Vine*, October 1997.

[53] *SMUMC News*, October 1993.

recently joined, or returned to Stewart Memorial. Alero Afe-juku, Kern Cox and Jai Harris related to the congregation their Christian journeys.[54]

Student Recognition Day

Student Recognition Day is an annual observance at Stewart Memorial. Its purpose is to recognize the students in our churches who are in college, and to encourage others to go to college to better prepare themselves to live in a changing order. In 1962, the student speaker for the occasion was Elaine Moore (Smith), a student at Bethune-Cookman College. She challenged young people "to make use of every available opportunity to become useful citizens." J. A. Adams, Jr., pastor, challenged the students to prepare themselves to dominate such evils as crime, disease, ignorance, poverty, and war. The congregation was warned that if these evils were not challenged successfully, they would destroy mankind.[55]

United Methodist Student Sunday was observed on December 31, 1972 with David Moore, a freshman at Bethune-Cookman presiding. The main speaker was Theodore Nicholson, Jr., a senior at Mainland High School. Other participants included: Ms Barbara Moore, Brenda and Saundra Nicholson of Bethune-Cookman College and Cynthia Curinton, of Spellman College and Herbert Thompson, Jr. of Father Lopez High School.[56]

David Moore, a medical student at Meharry Medical College presided over the Student Recognition Day of December 28, 1975. The theme was "The Unique Role of the Church in Christian Higher Education." The main speaker was Wayne I. Butler, a senior at Bethune-Cookman College. Other participants were John Leland Huger, freshman at Bethune-Cookman, Samuel Sharper, senior at BCC, Cynthia Curington senior at

---

[54]Church Bulletin.

[55]*Stewart Memorial Herald*, January 1962.

[56]Church Bulletin, December 1972.

Spellman, Herbert Thompson, junior at BCC and Ramona Lo
freshman at BCC.[57]

During the last two decades, Olivia Jones, Shirley Watts
Bing and S. Louise Rosemond have headed the Worship Committee.

---

[57]Church Bulletin, December 28, 1975.

Chapter 13

Nurture and Caring Ministry

The duty assigned to the Nurture and Caring Ministry is "to plan and implement programs related to the spiritual growth and special needs of the membership and others for building up the body of Christ." Under its jurisdiction are the health and welfare ministry, age-group ministries, scholarship, class leaders, and the grief ministries.[1]

Welcoming New Members into the Fold

Stewart Memorial maintains concern for those associated with it from birth to death. Many are the baptismal services which offer prayer for the newborn, and numerous are the funerals in which we say goodbye to those whom we love. Nurturing and caring ministries extend from the "cradle to the grave."

In 2006 there were two new additions to our church family through baptism: Kern Cox and James Williams. During the same year, four were funeralized: Mary Lucas Cook, Hildred

---

[1] Program Calendar and Membership Directory, 2001.

Stewart, Luvert G. Roberson and Charles W. Mathis.[2] In spite of the ratio of death to baptism shown above, Stewart Memorial continues to grow.

While a church is blessed to receive into its fold babies and infants, those persons are not fully associated with the church until they reach the age required for full membership. Through the process of confirmation, youthful members pass from the preparatory stage to full membership. That ritual has varied through the years, but generally, they respond to the question: "Will you be loyal to the United Methodist Church, and uphold it by your prayers, your presence, your gifts, and your service?" Rogers P. Fair, pastor, began his first confirmation class on March 4, 1973, with approximately 14 young and adult persons. Prior to their confirmation, the candidates were taught essential facts concerning the Methodist Church.[3]

The confirmation service on Sunday June 12, 1983, was preceded by a Friday night instructional session and confirmation supper with Ernest W. Newman, Deland District Superintendent, and the District Coordinator present for the occasion.[4]

As pastor, Kevin James welcomed new members at a New Members Breakfast at Quincy's Restaurant on April 25, 1998. As with previous confirmation programs, a series of learning experiences preceded the climaxing activity.[5]

The confirmation services of 2006 were unique inasmuch as its climaxing program was held as a part of the Easter morning services. Walter Monroe, pastor, led the congregation in celebrating the new birth that took place following the resurrection of Christ with the confirmation of twelve new members of Stewart Memorial. Those confirmed were: Kern Cox (Adult), Jonathan Davis, David Ellis (Adult), Erik Greer, Eric Polite, Marcus Ray, Michael Ray, Julian Smith, Brianna Thompson, Lenore Thompson, Stephanie Thompson, and Rashad Williams.

---

[2]Pastor's Report for 2006.
[3]Memo from Mrs. Agnes Fair.
[4]Letter to Mrs. Shirley Bing from Rev. Rogers P. Fair, March 25, 1983.
[5]Church Bulletin, April 19, 1998.

Prior to the Easter services, those who were confirmed were participants in several seminars related to the United Methodist Church and Stewart Memorial, in particular.[6]

Generally, the members of Stewart Memorial are professing or associate members. They usually are welcomed into the fold at the time of their affiliation with the church, or following their baptism. Occasionally they have been welcomed into membership as annual events. Typical of this was the New Members Dinner of December 13, 1985, in which the pastor, Rogers P. Fair, presided. Following dinner, several presentations were made:

- "The United Methodist Church as a Connectional Body," Richard V. Moore, Charge Lay Leader

- "The United Methodist Church and Black History," J. Otis Irvin, Retired UMC Minister

- "Local and District Structure," Rogers P. Fair, Pastor

- "The Council on Ministries," Phannye B. Huger.[7]

Health and Welfare Ministry

Because the health and welfare of the members are of major concern to Stewart Memorial, it developed a channel by which it can be kept informed of their well-being. A Health and Welfare Ministry was established for that purpose. In 1973 this ministry was chaired by Eloise Swilley,[8] and in 1993, it was headed by Hortense Mathis and Irene Steward.[9] In 1998 the Health and Welfare Ministry was headed by Minnie Harris, who described its work as ministering to the sick and shut-in through telephone

---

[6]Memorandum from Pastor's Office.

[7]Copy of Program.

[8]A Service of Consecration and Open House, Stewart Memorial United Methodist Church, April 15, 1973.

[9]Stewart Memorial United Methodist Church,100th Anniversary Celebration, March 14, 1993.

calls, visits, cards, fruit baskets, flowers, fragrances, assistance in delivering Holy Communion and providing Sunday dinners on designated Sundays. Taped sermons and tape players were provided as needed.[10] In 2006 that Ministry was headed by Annie M. Bell, Mary Slater and Mable Saxon.[11] Members of this ministry continue to visit or contact members of Stewart Memorial, whose names are on the Circle of Concern list, as well as those known to be ill. They deliver to them cards, flowers, monetary gifts and fruits to cheer their broken spirits.

Class Leaders of 1973

The chair of the Class leaders during 1973 was Mrs. Dufferin Harris, who often hosted meetings of the group in her home.

Class 1: Anthony M. Stephens
Class 2: Calvin Tynes
Class 3: Richard Bell
Class 4: Flossie Curinton
Class 5: Dufferin Harris
Class 6: John Gainey
Class 7: Dr. Richard V. Moore, Sr.
Class 8: C.S. Shears
Class 9: Ellouise Swilley
Class 10: C.W. Jenkins
Class 11: Margaret Bartley
Class 12: Samuel Sharper
Class 13: David Moore[12]

By 1993, the Class Leaders had changed drastically, with only Nathalie Jenkins and Margaret Bartley remaining in that position.

Class 1: Franklin Boston
Class 2: Minnie Harris

---

[10] Administrative Council, June 1998.

[11] List of Officers, 2006.

[12] A Service of Consecration and Open House, Stewart Memorial United Methodist Church, April 15, 1973.

Class 3: Johnnie Pride, Elizabeth Bell
Class 4: John Huger
Class 5: Thelma Irvin
Class 6: Jessie Childs, Senorita Locklear
Class 7: Henry T. Christian
Class 8: Eloise Snell, Jean McLean
Class 9: Nathalie Jenkins
Class 10: Margaret Bartley[13]

Gladys Greene recalled the pastor, Carrill Munnings, asking her to replace Eloise Snell as co-leader of Class Eight. She noted that as a newly appointed class leader, she underwent orientation under the pastor, and familiarized herself with her class members by hosting an acquaintance meeting at her home. Meetings were held quarterly and were under the guidance of the pastor. Scriptures were read and discussed by a worship leader and reacted to by members of the class. These classes continued under Joreatha M. Capers, who succeeded Munnings as pastor.[14]

Gladys Greene, one of the active co-leaders, described the activities of her class as:

> Responding to opportunities to exhibit the caring spirit through offering gift packages, hosting a baby shower for one of the families of the class, introducing new pastor to members, supporting programs sponsored by the Stewardship Committee and visiting members in hospitals and their homes.[15]

Class Eight, according to Mrs. Greene, consisted of thirty-seven members at the beginning of her tenure, including eight preparatory members. As she recalled, however, death, attrition,

---

[13] Stewart Memorial United Methodist Church,100th Anniversary Celebration, March 14, 1993.

[14] Memo from Mrs. Gladys Greene.

[15] Ibid.

relocation and at-large status reduced the size of her class. There were only nine members at the end of her tenure.[16]

Older Adult Ministries

Among the active members of Stewart Memorial are many older adults. They perform valuable services for the church, and they are deserving of good treatment from a church, which they served faithfully through the years. In 1996, Jean McLean, headed the Older Adults Ministry, and was dedicated to its effectiveness. She stated its purpose as follows:

> To become aware of the concerns and needs of the Older Adults in our congregation and our neighbors from other churches in our community, so we can reach out in love by caring and sharing as Christians and good neighbors. This program emphasis includes worship, prayer, scripture and a message of caring, sharing and fellowship.[17]

She noted the following activities for 1996:

- Apr 18: Get Acquainted Fellowship – A Daytona Beach Police Officer discussed scams that affect seniors. (48 present)

- Jun 22: Children and older Adults enjoyed a picnic of food and fellowship

- Sep 19: A Fall social with Kennetha Tsai giving a message on Restoration.

- Dec: A Senior Christmas Special (Scheduled)[18]

---

[16]Ibid.
[17]Administrative Council, June 1996.
[18]Ibid.

Young Adults Ministry

Young adults have contributed much to the well-being of Stewart Memorial. This group was especially active during the 1972-73 period, when the Young Active Christians of Stewart (YACS) made worthy contributions in several ways. One of its earlier efforts, under the presidency of Sandra Burney was the presentation of the Passion and Resurrection Pageant on Easter of 1972, which Joyce Elliott directed.[19] In June 1972, it showed concern for a struggling Sunday School by appointing a special committee, composed of Sandra Burney, Ann Whitehead, Peggy Brennon and Jessie Childs, to assist Margaret Bartley in her effort to build a better Sunday School.[20] On Feb 25, 1973, YACS celebrated its first anniversary in a four o'clock service with Rev. Neo Garvin speaker and the BCC Gospel Choir bringing music. Perhaps, one of its most recognized projects was the compiling and publishing of the Yearbook that accompanied the Service of Consecration and Open House on April 15, 1973. When Stewart Memorial moved into its present edifices, YACS' contribution was a new piano. In June 1973 Peggy Brennon replaced Sandra Burney as president.[21]

In 1997, not a part of YACS, a committee of young adults, composed of Juanita Sharper, Vandelyn Lee, Phyllis Jones and Minister David Allen, sponsored a reception for "Young Adults and Community Friends." The December 6 holiday reception provided a setting for these young people "to share testimonies and tap into a spiritual network of encouragement and support."[22]

---

[19]Church Bulletin, March 19, 1972.
[20]Church Bulletin, June 18, 1972.
[21]Church Bulletin, June 12, 1973.
[22]*The Vine*, December 1997.

Youth Ministry

According to the Book of Discipline, the youth ministry encompasses all concerns of the church and all activities by, with and for youth. It includes all persons from approximately 12 to 18 or, in terms of classes, students from 7th to 12th grade.[23]

The many activities of the youth of Stewart Memorial are discussed in Chapter 12 under the heading "Youth Fellowship and Other Youth Activities." This section is reserved for efforts to enhance the activities of the youth of the church.

One of the concerns of the church is the less than anticipated attendance of young people in worship services. As early as October 1992, Allen Sharper a high school student shared his views on that subject. He wrote in the *SMUMC News*:

> Satan has a grasp on many people, church people and the lost alike. Some reasons why church attendance is low for the youth include such reasons as they don't have to go to church to believe in God; others state they think church is stupid. Others prefer to stay home and sleep because they stayed up so late the day before church. People always have to make up reasons why they don't go to church...[24]

When the Vision 2000 Document was released in 1993, it listed developing a Youth Ministries as its fifth priority. The Committee envisioned an important role for the youth of the church. The document read in part:

> We are recommending that our annual budgetary planning include at least some minimal funding and scholarship assistance for youth participation in Deland District and Florida Conference youth

[23] *The Book of Discipline of the United Methodist Church*, 1996, 258-2.
[24] *SMUMC News*, October 1992.

events, and at the local church level, we are
recommending that our church develop an ongoing
schedule of Youth Impact dramas to attract other
youth to our relevant youth ministries.[25]

During his pastoral charge, Carrill Munnings was a strong
supporter of the youth program. In August 1993 he made this
appeal:

Let us prayerfully work together to support our
work of ministry toward our young people. As
I have said before, where our young people are
concerned, we must answer the question, "Is the
Young Person Safe?" This is the perennial question
of society. For none of us is safe if the young
person is not safe. At great risk is the safety of the
souls of the young in our immediate community.
Be prayerful, be involved, and most of all be an
example of Christ like living for our young people!
Amen.[26]

Through the years, the Youth Ministries have had strong
coordinators. In 1973 Iona Burney was coordinator of Youth
Ministries, and throughout the eighties Shirley Bing played a
leadership role. In 1993, youth leaders were Reginald King
and Joseph Ampiaw and in 2006 Wanda Pride.[27] In the various activities of the youth, parents and supporting Christians
gave strong support to the leaders of the Youth Ministries.

Children Ministry

The coordinator of Children Ministries is responsible for expos-
ing children to regular worship. A portion of the regular Sunday

---

[25] *Vision 2000*, July 12, 1993, 3.

[26] *SMUMC News*, August 1993.

[27] *Consecration* (1973), *Celebration* (1993), Bing's Files, and *Installation*
(2006).

Service, has on occasion, been devoted to a sermon for children. Several persons have performed the challenging task of conducting it. Historical records indicate that Eilean Leonard was in charge of that program in 1984, and conducted it until her illness prevented her from doing so.[28] She was replaced by Glenda Lewis, who continued the ministry until she left the city for employment in Washington, D.C. In 2005, in a program designed by Jessie Childs, several persons participated in the program. Often these children sermons were as informative to the general congregation as to the children. In 2006, the children attend "Children Church" which is under the direction of Rose Green Wilson.[29]

The children join with the youth of the church to form the children/youth choir, which is directed by Kevin Cooper and Janette Gibson. The children also are actively involved as acolytes and ushers.

Christmas and Easter are big celebrations for children, with special programs and activities arranged for those purposes. "Holy-Ween" is usually celebrated on October 31 with a party. Children are asked to wear Biblical attire and join the party of "Food, Fun, Films and Fellowship."[30] Children also have had the opportunity to travel. Fifteen children, along with parents visited Disney World. They also have visited Washington, DC, Atlanta, GA and other places.

Several persons have served as coordinator of Children Ministries, including: Olga Thompson who was serving in that capacity in 1973, Eilean Leonard (1984), Glenda Lewis and Wanda Pride (1993), and Janette Gibson (2006).

Like most of the major ministries of the church, the Nurture & Caring Ministry works closely with the others to achieve its purposes. Celestine Hinson chaired the 2006 ministry.

---

[28] *SMUMC News*, May 1984.
[29] Church Bulletin, September 3, 2006.
[30] Church Bulletin, October 22, 2006.

Chapter 14

Outreach Ministry

Stewart Memorial supports many outreach ministries through the United Methodist Church. It participates in the regular church observances, both financially and in awareness development. Perhaps the Methodist project to which it has given the strongest support is the Florida United Methodist Children's Home in Enterprise, Florida. A fifth Sunday offering is taken four times a year for that purpose. Before the merger of the Children's Homes in 1970, Stewart Memorial was a strong supporter of the Sarah Hunt Methodist Home.

The Halifax Urban Ministries, also, has been a constant recipient of support from Stewart Memorial. Leading in that drive was the head of missions. In 1973, Hortense Mathis was the chairperson for missions.[1] Later, Lillian Wisniewski held the position. In her 1998 report, she reported that her ministry was providing non-perishable food for the Halifax Urban Ministries monthly and assisting with the food preparation for the homeless. She also reported that members spent a day on the campus of the United Methodist Children's Home. Kay Wingard, the speaker for Mission Sunday, focused her presentation on sending men, women and children to help churches in other coun-

---

[1] A Service of Consecration and Open House, Stewart Memorial United Methodist Church, April 15, 1973.

tries. The Ministry also hosted Don Hill, a United Methodist missionary in the Congo in the 1960s.[2] In 2006, Mary Fears and Muriel J. Bartley headed the Mission Ministry. They sought to meet the needs of the hungry and homeless by promoting the "Ten–Ten-Ten" (10 number 10 cans by the 10th of each month) campaign on behalf of the Halifax Urban Ministries.[3] The Ministry on Mission supports many worthy causes, locally and beyond.

The church has responded to those affected by hurricanes, especially Andrew in 1992, the four storms that struck Florida in 2004 and Hurricane Katrina which devastated the upper Gulf Coast in 2005. Special offerings were taken.[4]

In addition to responding to the needs of others, the church seeks to respond to the needs of its members. The Disaster Response Ministry, which for many years was headed by James Huger, was chaired by Harold Heard in 2006.[5] In that position, the chairs kept the church informed about preparations for emergencies. This sub-ministry falls under the umbrella of the Nurture and Care ministry, chaired by Celestine Hinson. Members of the Preparedness Team include: Josselyn M. Bartley, Jessie Childs, Delores Davis, Franklin Boston, Joel and Mary Fears, Merceda Nicholson, Shelia Jackson and Celestine Hinson.[6]

Like many struggling institutions, Stewart Memorial has relied strongly on prayer, which has been uttered both privately and publicly. Public prayer meetings have been held at times in homes, but mostly in the church. They have at times been a thriving ministry, and at other times a struggling program with only three or four dedicated persons attending the services. As early as 1900, if not earlier, prayer meetings were held weekly.[7]

On October 18, 1972 after Prayer Meeting had ceased to

---

[2] Administrative Council, 1996.
[3] List of Officers for 2006, Regular Church Bulletins.
[4] Author's recollections.
[5] For Huger, see earlier directories; For Heard, see officers for 2006.
[6] Directory, 2007.
[7] *Daytona Gazette*, January 5, 1901.

exist for awhile, the pastor, Rogers P. Fair asked various persons and organizations to spearhead the prayerful effort. He insisted that "our church needs this hour of prayer." On the initial evening of prayer service the Voices of Joy Choir brought music. The hour was seen as a coming "together in prayer and thanksgiving to Almighty God for His goodness to us." Members were asked to pledge to attend this worthwhile service.[8]

In 2006, Juanita Sharper spearheaded the prayer advocacy. Prayer service is held every Wednesday.

Evangelism is a natural part of Stewart Memorial. Earlier histories refer to the summer revivals. Typical of the revivals is the one of April 9-12, 1979 conducted by visiting minister, William Ferguson with B. J. Moore, chair of Evangelism.[9] Juanita Sharper, who holds a lifetime membership and has been active in this field, recalled many of the old revivals and the in-house ones which preceded them.[10] Carrill Munnings, the pastor in 1994 recalled the spring revival of that year which was conducted by Cornelius Henderson, who later was to become Bishop. "He was kind enough to lend us his services for an old fashioned revival at Stewart Memorial which followed Religious Emphasis Week at Bethune-Cookman that year," said Munnings.[11]

The Scouting Program, which has existed for more than fifty years, and the Jump Start Program of 2000-2002 are discussed in the chapter on Stewart Memorial and the Community. Likewise, other outreach programs are included in the chapters on Stewart Memorial and Bethune-Cookman College; and Stewart Memorial and Ecumenical Ties.

Jessie Childs headed the 2006 Outreach Ministry.

---

[8]Church Bulletin, October 22, 1972.

[9]Directory, 2006.

[10]Conversation with Mrs. Sharper, July 1, 2007.

[11]e-mail from Rev. C. S. Munnings.

Chapter 15

Growth and Enrichment Ministry

Through the Growth and Enrichment Ministry the church seeks "to educate and strengthen ourselves [its members] for ministry to others in order that all will grow in the Christian faith and become disciples."[1] Although this ministry is of recent creation, Christian education has played a major role at Stewart Memorial since its infancy. In 1947, that function was under the direction of the Local Board of Education, chaired by James E. Huger.

Figure 15.1: Church School

Among those on the Board were William Slack, superintendent of the Church School; Virginia Brigety, the chair of the Commission on Good Literature; and heads of other auxiliaries. The Board was described as being

---

[1] *Program Calendar and Membership Directory*, 1998, p.3.

"responsible for the entire educational program of the church. Meeting at intervals in the operation of the total program of the church, this board keeps a close check upon the functions of the various organizations."[2]

In 1996, several areas of the Council on Ministries were combined to form the Growth and Enrichment Ministry. Among those were: the Church School, Vacation Bible School, resources, Disciple Bible Study, Bible Study, retreats and long range planning.[3]

Church School

According to the Book of Discipline, a church school should exist in every local church for the purpose of accomplishing the church's educational ministry. This challenge is given:

> The church school is challenged to nurture the skills of social interaction in keeping with our Christian tradition. Beginning in their early years, children should be nurtured to develop the attitudes and skills that enable them to seek nonviolent solutions. As an integral part of the curriculum, church schools shall teach the skills and practice of nonviolence as a powerful witness to Christian faith and an effective strategy for conflict resolution.[4]

Perhaps one of the oldest continuous educational programs of Stewart Memorial is the Church School, which existed from the founding of the church. Records are not available for the early years, but in 1945 the superintendent of the Church School was J.L. Slack, and one of its reliable teachers was Margaret Bartley.[5]

---

[2] *Handbook of Stewart Memorial Methodist Church, 1893 –1947.*
[3] *Program Calendar and Membership Directory*, 1998, p.4.
[4] *The Book of Discipline of the United Methodist Church, 1996.*
[5] *Handbook of Stewart Memorial Methodist Church, 1893 –1947.*

In 1970, the pastor praised Bartley for her outstanding work as superintendent. He noted that 78 persons were present at a recent Church School.[6] Three years later, the *Stewart Memorial UMC News* lauded her as she prepared to retire from the study program after twenty-two years of service. It noted:

> Many members of Stewart Memorial will take the nostalgic trip back through the years when our church was in need of strong and dedicated leadership.   In this area of our mission, Mrs. Bartley offered her service as a young woman with children of her own that she brought to Sunday School each week. We shall always remember with grateful hearts her sacrificial efforts to build the Sunday School, siphoning from her limited time as a wife, teacher, and mother, many hours of extra duty to keep the Sunday School alive and effective. She touched with great affection and understanding the lives of many young people who have grown to productive manhood and womanhood. Her mark will never be lifted from their lives.[7]

Margaret Bartley was replaced by Harry Burney, Jr. who in 1976 was still seeking support for the Church School. He wrote:

> I am certain that we are aware of the place of the Sunday School in the life of our church, and that you would want to see it grow. If you are this person, we need your help to keep our Sunday School alive. We need your attendance and participation at 9:30 each Sunday morning.[8]

In its July 12, 1993 report the Vision 2000 Committee listed as its third priority: To Revise Sunday School, noting, "Our

[6] Administrative Board, March 30, 1970.
[7] Stewart Memorial Herald, January 1973.
[8] Church Bulletin, September 28, 1976.

Christian Education in general needs revising to include new audio/visual teaching helps such as the video tape."[9]

Even though teachers have tried to enrich themselves, attendance has been low in recent years. Olive and Glenda Lewis represented Stewart Memorial at the 16th Annual Sunday School Teacher Weekend Retreat in Leesburg. The theme was "Teach to Reach." They received a wealth of information and new ideas that would help all age levels of our church school.[10] The Primary Sunday Class accompanied the Lewises to Mr. Gattis Pizza Parlor and played miniature golf at Castle Adventure next to the mall on January 25, 1992.[11]

In Jake Miller's argument for a stronger Church School, he maintained:

> Sunday School is internationalized, with the same lesson being taught each Sunday around the world by various denominations. One can meet a stranger on the bus and find that they can discuss the Sunday School lesson for the previous week, even though one is a Methodist and the other is a Baptist. Christians are brought closer together when they have lessons in common.

He further suggested that:

> A major purpose of Sunday School is to provide training which will enable members to better function as members of the larger church. Virtually every Sunday there are questions or statements listed in the book that relate to the church, at large. Typical of recent lessons was that of January 21, 2001, in which the questions were posed: What, if anything, has disturbed you about the new directions

---

[9] *Vision 2000*, July 12, 1993, 1.

[10] *SMUMC News*, October 1992, Vol. 2, No. 2.

[11] *SMUMC News*, February 11, 1992, Vol. 2, No. 2.

in church life, and what does your church do to celebrate with the stranger and with the new Christian?[12]

Through the years, Stewart Memorial has had some devoted
superintendents, including: J.S. Slack, Margaret Bartley, Harry
Burney, David Hinson, Cleo Higgins, Joseph Ampiaw, Willie
Scott, and Jake Miller.

In 2006 the Church School was continuing to function, but
mostly as an adult class. The children and youth attended the
Children Church. Samuel Sharper, Sr. was the teacher for the
adult class. Although reluctant to assume that role at the outset,
he enjoys the experience today. He sees teaching as an opportunity to increase his knowledge of the Bible, and to see it in a
practical sense.[13] Participating actively in the adult class during 2006 were three members of Stewart Memorial who had
exceeded the age of ninety: Gladys Greene, B.J. Moore, and
Eloise Snell. Also continuing to play an active role was Juanita
Sharper, whose membership in the church dates back to 1937,
and her involvement in Church School began almost simultaneously. Sharper advanced through all of the classes from the
primary to the Adult. She, like B.J. Moore, brought nine children to church School and continued the practice long after they
had reached adulthood.[14]

Once you have participated in church school, you remember the experience. In looking back over her Sunday School
experiences, Margaret Mitchell recalled:

> I really enjoyed my Sunday School time, because
> Mrs. Bartley was a good teacher, and looking back
> now, I am glad that mama made me go. I would not
> have changed one thing.[15]

---

[12]Statement on Sunday School by Jake Miller, 2000.

[13]Statement by Samuel Sharper.

[14]Comments of Mrs. Juanita Sharper and Mrs. B. J. Moore.

[15]Memo from Mrs. Margaret Mitchell.

Although she enjoyed Sunday School, there was one day, she would have preferred not being there. This is how she remembered it.

> One morning my mama sent me to Sunday School, and it had rained. There was a big puddle of water there on the side of the street. A car came by and ran over this puddle and water splashed all over my attire! Well, I ran back home, dripping with dirty water, just knowing that I was going to stay at home. I just knew that mama would take pity on me, and keep me home. Right? Wrong! Mama just made me change and sent me back on my reluctant way.[16]

Vacation Bible School

Vacation Bible School has been organized in several ways, including as a special entity of Stewart Memorial. As such, it has been directed by several people, including Celestine Hinson, one of the earlier organizers who sought to build on her experience as a child. She was aided by Jessie Childs and Phannye B. Huger, the chairperson of the Board of Ministry.[17] She was succeeded by such persons as Childs, Jake Miller, Jewel Hamm, Cleo Higgins, Joseph Ampiaw, and D' Mitri Cato Watson.

During the early 1980s, Sallie Shelton Culver developed a unified Vacation Bible School with First United Methodist.[18] In the early 2000s Jessie Childs led in developing a partnership summer program with Shiloh Baptist.[19] Stewart Memorial has also participated in a city-wide program, under the auspices of the Black Clergy Alliance. In this Vacation Bible program, Stewart Memorial is the home of the middle school students.[20]

[16]Ibid.
[17]Shirley Moore/Shirley Bing, Update of History of Stewart Memorial.
[18]Memo from Mrs. Sallie Shelton Culver.
[19]Conversation with Mrs. Jessie Childs.
[20]Church Bulletin, July 2, 2006.

Bible Studies

Through the years, Bible study has taken several forms. In the early years, it took place both in homes and at the church. Some lessons have been based on certain books of the Bible, while others have covered the entire Bible. While pastor, Joreatha Caper directed a one-year study of the Bible, examining from Genesis to Revelations. Michael Frazier also sought to study the entire Bible, but over a period of years. Some studies have been pastor-led, while others have been led by members. In 2006 there were two regular Bible classes: a Tuesday Morning Bible Class led initially by B. J. Moore and a Tuesday evening Bible Class under the direction of Juanita Sharper. Later, the classes were taught by Pastor Monroe and Minister Sedrick Harris, respectively.

During the summer of 2006, Sedrick Harris coordinated a six-week Bible class for men. The two days per week class for six weeks had the following purposes:

- Discover how scripture can specifically speak to the issues of men.

- Assist in the development of daily Bible reading.

- Help begin the process of understanding spiritual ramifications for natural actions.

- Help understand our Godly role within the family, the church and society.

- Establish a foundation that will build an effective cross-generational relationship.[21]

The Class explored the following topics: masculinity, accountability, discipleship, attitude adjustment, men at work, and for men only.

---

[21] Bible Class brochure.

During the fall of 2001, Sedrick Harris conducted a Bible class for young adults which was composed mostly of college students.[22]

For three years, Stewart Memorial conducted a special type of Bible Class, known internationally as Disciple Classes. That subject will be treated under that heading.

Key 73

Key 73 was defined as a "spiritual uplifting" program that consisted of Bible Study, personal encounter, and discussion. It was under the direction of Florence L. Roane.[23] Preparation for this unique project was begun in 1972 with Rev. Fair leading in the study of the Book of Acts.[24] The second phase of Key 73 focused on a study of the Book of Romans.[25] It also was a period devoted to preparation for witnessing and witnessing, itself. The Voices of Joy Gospel Choir, usually brought music for the program.[26]

Disciple Class

The Disciple Program, an international program, was introduced to Stewart Memorial United Methodist Church in September 1995. As a prelude to launching this study program, Dr. Capers proposed sending eight people to the Disciple One seminar in Atlanta for preparation as teachers.[27] Upon their return, the program was put into operation. Sallie Shelton Culver and Dr. Capers coordinated the basic Stewart Memorial Class, Drs. Cleo Higgins and Sheila Flemming directed the Bethune-Cookman class, Minister Lynn Thompson and Mrs.

---

[22] Church Bulletin.

[23] Church Bulletin, April 1, 1973.

[24] Church Bulletin, Oct 8, 1972.

[25] Church Bulletin, Jan 21, 1973.

[26] Church Bulletin, Jan 28, 1973.

[27] Administrative Board *Action News*, July 10, 1995.

Thompson coordinated the class for couples and Sheila Flemming directed the youth class. There were twenty participants in the three adult classes who completed Disciple One course: "Becoming Disciples Through Bible Study."[28]   At the close of Disciple One, Mrs. Shelton Culver was sent to Atlanta to pursue training for the Disciples Two program. Upon her return she organized a class, and was assisted by Dr. Jake Miller, who later attended the Atlanta Seminar to be certified to teach Disciple Two.[29] Nine of the graduates of Disciple One enrolled the following year and completed Disciple Two: "Into the Word Into the World."[30]

According to the Disciple Handbook, "underlying the development of Disciple is the assumption that people are hungry for the word of God, for fellowship in prayer and study, and for a sense of appropriate ministry as baptized, believing, committed Christians." Virtually, all participants in the program expressed enthusiasm over what was learned and their interaction with other classmates. Below are some of the comments. Olivia Durant, a member of Highlands Presbyterian Church wrote:

The desire to learn more grows and grows; thus, I am becoming more disciplined in study, more thoughtful in deliberation.[31]

Jimmie Crawford-Rhinehart wrote:

My story is one of enlightenment. I came out of darkness, which was the lack of knowledge about the word and how to apply this knowledge into the world.[32]

Herbert Harris wrote:

---

[28] Administrative Board, July 15, 1996.
[29] Author's recollections.
[30] *The Vine*, July 1998.
[31] *Disciple: Our Story*, 5.
[32] Ibid., 17.

A Disciple is a follower. In order to be a disciple,
one must humble himself to leadership. The qualities of a disciple should be obedience, prayerful
thinking, patience, availability, enthusiasm, sincer-
ity, understanding, sensitivity and love in a Christian life. The disciple must be a follower of Jesus.[33]

Hildred Stewart expressed her feeling of becoming a disciple in these words:

During my journey, I could feel the touch of spiritual growth and enlightenment. About halfway on
the journey, I became more intense and more involved in what was the real reason for feeling so
full of the spirit that was being passed on from one
classmate to the other. We bonded and found ourselves filled with love for one another. Thus, the
journey continued for 32 weeks. We are now a
happy family.[34]

Seminars and Workshops

Regardless of how effective we are in working for God, we still
can improve. That is one reason for workshops and seminars.
With that thought in mind, Dr. Rogers P. Fair invited Dr. Cornelius Henderson, chairman of the General Board of Evangelism, to conduct a seminar on evangelism at Stewart Memorial,
February 18, 1972. Mrs. Bobbie Caruthers, chairman of the
local work area on evangelism coordinated the seminar.[35] Not
every seminar was conducted by a specialist. On July 31, 1972,
the church conducted a two-hour seminar on the structure of the
church. Officers, committee members and all interested parties
were invited to participate in this seminar. The announcement

---

[33] Ibid., 11.

[34] Ibid., 19.

[35] *SMUMC* Observes Race Relations Day, February 13, 1972.

read: "We shall be discussing in everyday language what our church is, and how we can promote its mission."[36]

Shortly after Carrill Munnings assumed the pastoral charge, he organized a four-week seminar for officers of Stewart Memorial. The first session convened on September 29, 1992, and two hour meetings were held weekly for the three Tuesdays.[37]

The Library

The church is a place of learning as well as a place of worship. Consistent with that belief, Stewart Memorial has sought to provide useful literature for its parishioners. The 1947 handbook referred to the Commission on Good Literature as:

The commission, headed by Mrs. Virginia Brigety, sees to it that Stewart Memorial keeps abreast of the latest in religious literature. And further, it sees to it that organizations in the church take advantage of the wealth of literature published by the Methodist Publishing House."[38]

Several attempts have been made to establish a library (learning resource center) for Stewart Memorial. In 1973, the Committee on Nominations and Personnel nominated Nelse Pettway to be the librarian. Among those persons making or announcing intention of contributing books were Phannye Huger and Rogers P. Fair.[39] Likewise, the Administrative Board, in its October 29, 1973 meeting, authorized Mable Christian to use the temporary choir room as a library.

Even though efforts were made to sustain a library, the attempts were not successful. In an effort to make the library a reality, the Administrative Board, on April 10, 1995, approved a motion calling for the use of the Rosa Brooks Room as a library. Simultaneously, it set up a committee to make the ministry operative. The committee was composed of Mable Chris-

---

[36]Church Bulletin, July 23, 1972.

[37]*SMUMC News*, October 1992.

[38]*Handbook of Stewart Memorial Methodist Church, 1893 –1947*, 6.

[39]Consecration, 29, (*SMUMC News*, August 1973).

tian, Thelma Irvin, Mary J. Fears, and Gladys Greene.[40] After
being designated librarian, Gladys Greene catalogued the books
which had been given and purchased.

Working in cooperation with the ministry of Education, the
library prepared an educational program for 1996-97. Working
on the committee, which proposed the program were Cleo Higgins, Sallie Shelton Culver and Gladys Greene. As planned, the
program consisted of the following presentations:

- Dec. 9, 1996: "Kwanzaa," Judge Hubert Grimes

- Jan. 13, 1997: "Martin Luther King Trilogy," Lillian Wisnewski

- Feb. 10, 1997: "Black History Month," Sheila Flemming

- Mar. 10, 1997: "African-American History and Culture," Larry Wesley

- Apr. 14, 1997: "Social Life and Customs of Africa," Gladys Greene

- May 12, 1997: "African Heritage: Crossing the Waters to New Shores," Johnson Akinleye

- June 9, 1997: "African Heritage: International Festival," Thelma Irvin/Greater Friendship Baptist Church Praisers

- Sep. 8, 1997: "Poetry Recital," Cleo S. Higgins & Josephine Kennedy

- Oct. 13, 1997: "The Impact of the United Nations on African Americans and Africa," Jake C. Miller

- Nov. 10, 1997: "The Church of the Future," Minister David Allen.[41]

[40]Catalogue of Donated Resources 1995-96.
[41]Growth and Enrichment Files.

These second-Monday evening programs, which were begun in December 1996 by the Library Resource Committee and the Area of Education, were successful. When the ministries were reorganized, the Growth and Enrichment Ministry assumed responsibility for the program in October 1997. The programs continued until the summer of 2000.

Keeping the Church Informed

Through the years the church has been informed of its activities by announcements in the weekly bulletins and by various newsletters. The following have existed since 1962:

- *The Stewart-Memorial Herald,*

- *Stewart Memorial United Methodist Church News,*

- *The Administrative Board Action News,*

- *The Vine,*

- *The Stewart Memorial Newsletter, and*

- *The Stewart Memorial Good News Journal.*

The 2006 Growth and Enrichment Ministry was headed by Mary Alice Smith.

Chapter 16

Events Ministry

The Events Ministry plans and implements picnics, banquets, birthday breakfasts and special days, including receptions to welcome new pastors and events to bid farewell to retiring pastors, and those who have been assigned to different charges. Receptions have also been given for graduates and members of the church who retired from their places of work. The Committee, co-chaired by Jessie Childs and Shelia Jackson, perceived its duties to be:

> To plan and implement activities which support the ministry of the church through caring and sharing.

> To promote the involvement of many members of the church in special events, both in leadership roles and individual participation.

> To support committees in the implementation of programs.[1]

Numerous events are given at the church, but not necessarily sponsored by this ministry. They are discussed, however, under the heading of events. Typical of the banquets given were those honoring members of the church. A discussion of three of them follows:

---

[1]Events Ministry Report to Administrative Council, October 21, 1998.

Honors Banquets

Three honors banquets were given to honor members of Stewart Memorial and members selected from community churches. The first one was given on February 9, 1996, at the Palmetto Women's Club. Those honored were: Margaret Bartley, Shirley Watts Bing, Franklin D. Boston, Sr., Sallie Shelton Culver, Joel Fears, Sr., Gladys M. Greene, Thelma Hall, Glenda Lewis, Olive Lewis, B. J. Moore, Samuel Sharper, Sr., and Toni D. Stewart. The speaker for this occasion was Attorney Ruby Burrows McZier, a member of Stewart Memorial, who resides in Washington, DC.[2]

The Second Honors Banquet was held February 28, 1997, with David C. Hinson, the Volusia County Secondary Principal of the year, 1996 – 1997 speaker. Honorees were: Minnie Harris, John Heath, Lucy Heath, Shelia Jackson, Rev. Kevin M. James, Bettye A. Johnson, Jake C. Miller, Wanda A. Pride, Juanita Sharper and Minister Lynn W. Thompson. Youth members honored were Dedra Jackson and William "Jeff " Smith. The occasion also was used as a time to pay tribute to persons from community churches. Among those honored were: Bennie Tooley, Greater Friendship Baptist; Patricia Jones, Mt. Carmel Missionary Baptist; Gertrude Smith, St. Timothy's Episcopal; Dr. Cleo Higgins, Stewart Memorial United Methodist; Henry Oliver, Mt. Zion A.M.E.; Ruth Hankerson, New St. James Baptist; and Johnny MacDonald, Shady Grove Baptist.[3]

The Third Honors Banquet honored those members of Stewart Memorial who had held membership for more than fifty years. The occasion was a part of the celebration of the 105th anniversary of the church. Those honored included Bertha Baker, who held membership for 88 years, Dorothy Perkins (68), James E. Huger, Sr. (61), Mrs. Sarah Burns (61), Margaret Bartley (61), Thelma Hall (60), Juanita Sharper (60), Lorenzo Gamble (59), Eloise Edward Snell (59), Phannye

[2]Honors Banquet, Printed Program, February 9, 1996.
[3]Honors Banquet, Printed Program, February 28,1997.

B. Huger (56), and Delores Davis (53). Also, honored at the
banquet were persons selected by their churches for honors.
They included: Thelma Alderman, St Timothy Episcopal
Church; Shirley Bing, Stewart Memorial United Methodist
Church; Valetta Butler, Greater Friendship Baptist Church;
Ruth Hankerson, New St James; Carolyn Johnson, Hope Fel-
lowship; Dorothy Thomas, Shiloh Missionary Baptist Church
and Shirley A. White, New Mt. Zion Baptist Church.[4]

Welcoming and Farewell Receptions

A hospitable environment exists at Stewart Memorial, and
nowhere was that more evident than the welcoming receptions
for in-coming pastors. Likewise, the congregation has been
equally hospitable in saying farewell to pastors who were
ending their charges. In recent years, Stewart Memorial bade
farewell and expressed best wishes to Alfonso Delaney, Carrill
Munnings, Joreatha Capers and Kevin James as they moved
on to other positions in Methodism. For Eddie J. Rivers and
Rogers P. Fair the receptions were somewhat different, since
both previously had served Stewart Memorial for three pastoral
charges.

Birthday Breakfast

In 1973, under the pastorate of Rev. Fair, the monthly Birthday Breakfast was launched. This hour of fellowship was sponsored by members who celebrated birthdays during the month
being observed. In addition to partaking of a delicious morning
meal, those who attended participated and observed a program
planned by the host group. Also, as a part of the occasion, a
person or group, usually, was honored. The monthly birthday
celebration, a small group activity, provided an opportunity for
members of Stewart Memorial to become better acquainted with

---

[4]Honors Banquet, Printed Program, February 27, 1998.

each other. Guests from the church and the community were invited to the breakfast.[5]

Through the years the Birthday Breakfast underwent several changes. By 1992 emphasis was not only placed on a fellowship of members who had a common birthday month, but also on raising money to assist the sick and shut-in.[6]

In 1993, the monthly birthday observance was known as the Quarterly Pastor's Birthday Breakfast Ministry. Jacques Hodge was chairperson and the members were Henry T. Christian, Andy Jackson, Dewey Ruff, Thelma Hall, Hortense Mathis, Jean McLean and Irene Steward.[7]

In 1998, the committee for the quarterly birthday observance was headed by Harold Rhodes, and the members were Joel Fears, Sr., John R. Heath, Andy Jackson, Sr. Hortense Mathis, Jean McLean, Dorothy Perkins, Johnnie Pride and Dewey Ruff. Mclean, Mathis and Shirley Watts-Bing were in charge of the arrangements and preparation of the food. In order to better facilitate the activities, captains and co-captains for the various months were appointed. They were:

January: George Whitehead
February: Margaret Watson
March: Lucy Heath
April: Bettye Johnson
May: Jean McLean
June: Thelma Irvin
July: Toni Stewart & Shelia Jackson
August: Cleo Higgins & Joel Fears
September: George Whitehead & Merceda Nicholson
October: Elaine Sharper & Amelia Colston[8]

In 2006, the Quarterly Pastor Birthday Breakfast was under

[5] Author's recollections.
[6] *SMUMC News* Vol. 2, No 11, November 1992).
[7] Stewart Memorial United Methodist Church,100th Anniversary Celebration, March 14, 1993.
[8] Program Calendar and Membership Directory, 1998, 11.

the umbrella of the Events Ministry, headed by Celestine Hinson.[9]

Graduation/Retirement Reception

The Graduation/Retirement Reception is an activity held during the early part of the summer to pay tribute to those who have graduated from high school, college or graduate/professional school. The occasion, also, is used to honor those who have retired from their chosen occupations. Typical of such affairs was the one of December 6, 1989, honoring the retirements of Geraldine Griggs, Dr. Cleo Higgins, John Heath and Charles Mathis.[10]

Fellowship Social and Dinners

Fellowship activities have been sponsored by many groups, but for consistency, they are discussed under the heading of Events Ministry. Illustrative of that point, was the Family Fellowship Dinner of December 12, 1971, planned by the Family Ministries headed by Jennie Nicholson.[11] For the Fellowship Hour of Sunday, January 7, 1973, the congregation was invited to "come, eat, and chat in this beautiful edifice and then take a tour of its facilities." Thelma Hall and Juanita Sharper, co-chairpersons of the Dinner Committee planned a dinner for May 13, 1973, to coincide with the Cornerstone Laying.[12] Fellowship Dinners continue to be utilized by a variety of groups to achieve their purposes. The Stewardship Committee hosted a "Stewardship Dinner Celebration" for the membership of Stewart Memorial On May 29, 1994.[13]

Shelia D. Jackson chaired the 2006 Events Ministry.

---

[9]Program Calendar and Membership Directory, 2007.

[10]Printed Program.

[11]Church Bulletin, November 7, 1971

[12]Church Bulletin, May 6, 1973.

[13]Author's recollections.

Chapter 17

United Methodist Women

According to the *Book of Discipline*, the United Methodist Women shall be:

> a community of women whose purpose is to know God and to experience freedom as whole persons through Jesus Christ, to develop a creative supportive fellowship, and to expand concepts of mission through participation in the global ministries of the Church.[1]

The United Methodist Women's organization is a recent one, having been built on earlier women's organizations. According to historical accounts, a forerunner of this organization was the Women's Society of Christian Service, of which Selena Clemmons was the local president in 1947. Another women's organization of that time was the Wesleyan Guild, which was headed by Bertha Slack (Baker).[2]

Through the years, the Women's Society of Christian Service (United Methodist Women) was active in promoting Christian endeavors at Stewart Memorial. It has sponsored such activities as Mother's Day observances, the Week of Denial and

---

[1] *Book of Discipline*, 258C, art 3.
[2] *Handbook of Stewart Memorial Methodist Church, 1893 -1947.*

Prayer, and Bible Study utilizing a series on "Christian Being and Christian Doing."[3] It also sponsored many fellowship
activities, such as Christmas teas, garden affairs, and church
outings at Tomoka Park. The organization has had many active leaders including Hazelean McLendon, Portia Jones, Florence Roane, Henrine Ward Banks, Margaret Bartley, Beverly
V. Smith, Melvina Nagbe and Amelia Colston.[4]

Through its various activities, United Methodist Women has
sought to enhance Christian unity. Typical of its ecumenical focus was the tea given by the organization at the home of Margaret Gibbs on June 12, 1969. Invited to that affair were fifteen women from the Riverside Presbyterian Church.[5] This
affair was not an exceptional one since the United Methodist
Women of Stewart Memorial had developed a pattern of inviting guests from other churches to its teas. Attending the Annual
Tea on June 23, 1991, were members of the United Methodist
Women of First United Methodist Church of Ormond Beach,
Florida, Larry Hyde and Frances Strachen of St Timothy Episcopal Church and Cynthia Lewis of Tubman King Church of
Christ.[6]

Consistent with the *Book of Discipline*, United Methodist
Women of Stewart Memorial seeks "to give visible evidence
of oneness in Christ by uniting in fellowship and service with
other Christians."[7] Included among the organizations in which
it holds membership is Church Women United. This organization, which Agnes Fair headed in 1990,[8] was hosted by the
UMW of Stewart Memorial on November 1, 1974,[9] and on October 11, 1991.[10] Representatives from several area churches

---

[3] Administrative Board, October 31, 1966.
[4] Review of Administrative Board Cumulative Minutes.
[5] Administrative Board, June 12, 1969.
[6] Administrative Board, July 1991.
[7] *Book of Discipline*, 1317.9.
[8] *SMUMC News*, November 1991.
[9] Administrative Board, September 30,.1974.
[10] *SMUMC News*, November 1991.

attended.

Members of the United Methodist Women of Stewart Memorial have been active in the Deland District Organization. In 1974, Henrine Banks was the first African American elected president of the organization.[11] Melvina Nagbe was elected to head the organization in 1991.[12]

Women of Stewart Memorial have played active roles in the Deland District Meetings of the United Methodist Women. Paulette Monroe was elected president of the Florida Conference of Methodist Women in 2004. In her greetings after being elected president, she cited the following as goals she anticipated achieving:

- To launch a two-year United Methodist Women Membership Campaign in the Florida Conference,

- To help each District develop and implement a Committee on the Charter for Racial Policy.

- To strengthen channels of communication between conference, district, unit officers and unit members by 2007.[13]

As president, she has had an active term, preparing Missions Schools in St Petersburg in 2005, and at Florida Southern in Lakeland in 2006. She looks forward to the School of Missions at Bethune-Cookman in 2007.[14]

Members of the United Methodist Women of Stewart Memorial have sought to expand their focus by partaking of experiences beyond the Daytona Beach area. Four representatives—Margaret Bartley, Eloise Edwards (Snell),

---

[11]"Henrine Ward Banks Dead at 73," *Daytona Evening News*, April 24, 1980.

[12]*SMUMC News*, November 1991.

[13]Comments from Mrs. Paulette Monroe.

[14]Administrative Board, July 11, 1967.

Mary Morse and Alicia Floyd—were participants in the School of Mission in Lakeland in 1967.

Stewart Memorial sent even a larger delegation to the observance of the Tenth Annual Conference of United Methodist Women, which met at Florida Southern College in Lakeland on November 5-6, 1983. Participants in the gathering of more than a thousand were: Margaret Bartley, Shirley Watts-Bing, Marie Bolen, Eloise Edwards (Snell), Thelma Hall, Lucile Jones, Hazaleen McLendon, Ruth Neal, Mable Saxon, Beverly Smith, and Eloise Williams.[15]

Among the 2400 delegates to the 1987 South Eastern Jurisdiction meeting in Biloxi Mississippi were Margaret Bartley, Melvena Nagbe and Beverly Smith.[16]

Perhaps, one of the most important gatherings of Methodist women took place in Orlando, Florida on May 14-17, 1998. Margaret Bartley, Muriel J. Bartley, Shirley W. Bing, Sheila Flemming and Melvena Nagbe were among the more than 12,000 United Methodist women who convened in the United Methodist Women Assembly.[17]   The purpose of the organization is "to foster spiritual growth, develop leaders and advocate for social justice." According to the handout, "they brought materials to create hundreds of quilts for poor children and truckloads of relief supplies for people who have been displaced by natural disasters and war."[18]

The United Methodist Women and its forerunner have reflected an interest in international concerns. Illustrative of that was Henrine Ward Banks' participation in the Women's Committee on the International Institute for Women of Japan, a Methodist sponsored organization which encourages interests of church groups and women in the education of Japanese women.[19]

---

[15]*SMUMC News* (Undated) Bing's file.

[16]"Community News" *Daytona Times*, March 21, 27, 1987.

[17]Press Release (undated).

[18]Ibid.

[19]Banks (1980).

The United Methodist Women joined more than a million other United Methodist Women in celebrating the 20th birthday of the organization. The local organization held its celebration during the regular worship services September 27, 1992. The main speaker for the occasion was Mary Alice Smith, professor/director of Student Support Service, Bethune-Cookman College (University).[20]

The 2007 officers of the United Methodist Women of Stewart Memorial are:

President: Barbara Blossom

Vice President: Janice Walton

Secretary: Jai Harris

Treasurer: Atty. Alero Afejuku

Secretary of Program Research: Delores Davis & Fannie Rhodes

Chairman of Nomination: Celestine Hinson

Coordinator of Spiritual Growth: Mary Alice Smith.[21]

---

[20] *SMUMC News*, October 1992.

[21] Program Calendar and Membership Directory, 2007.

Chapter 18

United Methodist Men

> The United Methodist Men shall be a creative sup-
> portive fellowship of men who seek to know Je-
> sus Christ, to grow spiritually, and to seek daily his
> will. Its primary purpose is to declare the centrality
> of Christ in the lives of men and in all their rela-
> tionship.[1]

At Stewart Memorial, Texas Adams (1876-1957) was one
of the pioneers in men's work, serving as president of the
Methodist Men, which later became the United Methodist Men.
Working closely with him was Anthony Stevens, Sr., who was
referred to in the handbook as "an outstanding promoter." In
the forties, the organization had more than fifty members, and
it held meetings twice monthly. An assortment of speakers
usually addressed the group.[2]

In earlier years, Methodist Men's Day was a standard feature at Stewart Memorial. Typical of the programs presented
was a panel discussion of four invited community leaders on
February 22, 1970. The theme was: "God's Call and Man's Response." Men invited to speak were: Frank Barnes, an educator;

---

[1] *Book of Discipline*, 259.2.
[2] *Handbook of Stewart Memorial Methodist Church, 1893 –1947.*

Ernest Cook and R. J. Gainous, college officials; and Laurence Wesley, Sr. a business man.[3]

Fellowship has always been an important part of the United Methodist Men's program. In December 1971, a fellowship dinner followed the Methodist Men's Day observance. It permitted persons attending the affair to spend quality time with the guest speaker.[4]

"Fish and Grits suppers" were common occurrences, also. On November 12, 1972, such an event was given to motivate the men of Stewart Memorial, and to provide a fellowship activity for persons attending the Task Force of Key 73, a Bible Study group which held meetings on Sunday evenings.[5]

On the program of March 11, 1973, Clyde Briggs, Theodore Jones, Herbert Harris, R.J. Gainous and Harry Burney, Jr. were participants, and Laurence Wesley, local businessman, was the speaker.[6] Later in 1973, the United Methodist Men sponsored an informal fellowship hour following the Father's Day program of June 17, 1973, in which Dr. William Stewart, president of Edward Waters College was the speaker.[7]

Similar programs continued through the seventies and eighties. The Annual United Methodist Program of 1992 was unique, inasmuch as it could be considered a salute to African-American history, and a challenge for Christian men to make their impact felt. The main speaker for this January 24 program/dinner was the Honorable John L. Smart, retired chaplain of the U. S. Air Force, member of the United Methodist Men, Deland District and mayor of Lake Helen. The speaker emphasized that we should be thankful that we can sing, "Praise God From Whom All Blessings Flow." Following the address, the congregation had an opportunity to fellowship at the Dinner.[8]

---

[3] Administrative Board, January 5, 1970, 113.

[4] Administrative Council, November 1, 1971.

[5] Administrative Council, November 12 1972

[6] Church Bulletin, March 11, 1973.

[7] Administrative Council, June 17, 1973.

[8] *SMUMC News*, February 1992.

In addition to its special programs, United Methodist Men meets monthly, and occasionally, has guest speakers. On August 21, 1997, Jose Hernandez, a professor of education at Bethune-Cookman College discussed his findings on a research project entitled: "The Influence of Religious Practices of African-American Men over 65 Years of Age on Health and Well Being.[9] On March 18, 1999, Regina Thompson, Patient Education Unit of Halifax Hospital, discussed diabetes.[10] Speakers for the regular meetings also included members. On September 18, 1997, Andy Jackson, president, related some of his experiences in regard to his coin collecting.[11]

The United Methodist Men of the Florida Conference holds quarterly district meetings, and usually Stewart Memorial is well represented. The local chapter not only sends representatives to District meetings, it has, on occasion, hosted them. While there probably were more meetings, available records indicate that Stewart Memorial hosted the Deland District United Methodist Men on October 31, 1974, January 26, 1989 and January 1991. Pastor Eddie J. Rivers of Stewart Memorial extended an invitation in December 1988 which read: "It becomes my pleasure to invite all members of the United Methodist Men of the Deland District to Stewart Memorial United Methodist Church. I can assure you that you are welcome."[12] On the January 1991 visit, Allen Harrell, area manager of Sears was the main speaker, and the Bethune-Cookman College Chorale provided the music. Stewart Memorial's hospitality was warmly applauded.[13]

Men from Stewart Memorial have been active participants in its district, state and national conferences. Richard V. Moore, charge lay leader and an active local United Methodist Men leader, attended the National Conference of Methodist Men at

---

[9]Minutes, United Methodist Men (UMM) Meeting, August 21, 1997.
[10]UMM, March 18, 1999.
[11]UMM, September 18, 1997.
[12]Dr. Eddie J. Rivers Letter to UMM District Office, December 1988.
[13]*SMUMC News*, June 1991.

Purdue University, July 9-11, 1965. Also, as a member of the program committee, he presided over one of the sessions. Harrison DeShields, president of the local chapter of the United Methodist Men (UMM), also attended.[14] Joel Fears, a longtime leader of the UMM, attended the national meeting in 1969.

Andy Jackson and Joel Fears participated in the All Men and Clergy meeting of the Florida Conference in Orlando, FL.[15] Franklin Boston, Sr., Joel Fears, Sr., John Heath and Andy Jackson, Sr. attended the Bishop's Invitation for Christ's Men on July 11, 1998, and again in 2000.[16] Likewise, they and Michael Ray were participants in the Rally for Christ in Tallahassee, August 10, 2002.[17]

Members of the United Methodist Men do more than attend meetings. They perform a variety of functions. Perhaps, their most important project is sponsoring the Anthony Stephens Scouting Troop 108, which is more than fifty-two years old. Throughout the years several men have taken leading roles in the program, including Anthony Stephens, William McMillan, Neil Crosslin, Charles Cherry, Joel Fears, William Bell and Minister Willie Scott.[18] (The Scouting program will be discussed under a different heading).

Another program sponsored by the United Methodist Men, which was directed at the male youth of the church, was the "Boys to Men." At our first discussion, Mary Fears made a presentation.[19] The second activity was a Pancake Breakfast on March 1, 2002, which included a talk by Raymond D'Adesky, a local pediatrician.[20]

The United Methodist Men organization performs several tasks for the church, including serving as pallbearers for

---

[14] Administrative Board, July 5, 1965.
[15] UMM, February 28, 2002.
[16] UMM, August 19, 2000.
[17] UMM, August 15, 2002.
[18] *SMUMC News*, October 1993.
[19] UMM, February 17, 2000.
[20] UMM, February 28, 2002.

funerals, preparing meals for visiting groups or for special occasions, parking cars, and performing other duties at the Florida Methodist Children's Home in Enterprise, Florida.[21] It also contributes regularly to church rallies—Men's and Women's Days. It also has sought to meet the needs of the church by purchasing items like a tape duplicator which is used to make available sermons and programs to those who are not able to attend.[22] One of the United Methodist Men's more attractive activities is the annual summer fish fry, which provides an opportunity for church members and guests to fellowship.[23]

The organization has been led by such devoted leaders as Texas A. Adams, Harrison DeShields, Joel Fears, Harry Burney, Jr., John Heath, Attorney Roland Blossom, James Burgess and Andy Jackson.[24] Each president has had his unique style. DeShields selected a cabinet to help him with his program, including:

Program Chairman: Willie McLendon
Devotion Chairman: H. C. Harris
Project Chairman: Hurcules Swilley
Membership Chairman: J. Griffen Greene
Attendance Chairman: William Pierce
Publicity Chairman: James E. Huger
Reporter Chairman: James R. Greene

The officers for 2006 were:
President: Andy Jackson, Sr.
Vice President: John Heath
Secretary: Jake C. Miller
Charter Secretary: Joel Fears, Sr.
Treasurer: Frank Boston, Sr.

---

[21] UMM, April 15, 1999.
[22] *SMUMC News*, June 1998.
[23] See Directories.
[24] Consensus of members.

Chapter 19

Youth Fellowship and Related Youth Activities

According to the Book of Discipline:

> The youth ministry encompasses all concerns of the Church and all activities by, with and for youth. It includes all persons from approximately 12 to 18 or in terms of classes, students from 7th to 12th grade.[1]

While the major emphasis here is on the United Methodist Youth Fellowship and the organizations which preceded it, attention will be given to youth activities, generally.

A review of the membership roster of Stewart Memorial will reveal many members who affiliated with it during their childhood. They enjoyed such rich experiences as Church School and the Epworth League/United Methodist Youth Fellowship. The Church School is discussed in the chapter on Growth and Enrichment. Attention here will be given to the United Methodist Youth Fellowship and the organizations which led up to it.

---

[1] *Book of Discipline*, 1996.

The Epworth League was one of the earliest youth organizations of Stewart Memorial. While there are no records available concerning its activities, it apparently was a viable organization in 1901, since at that time it hosted the Sunday School and Epworth League Convention of the Jacksonville District of the Florida Conference of the Methodist Episcopal Church.[2]

Reflecting on it in 1937, Sarah Burns recalled that her sister, Harriet Bazzell was president. Working along with her were Frances Mae Kelley, Georgia Kelley, Catherine Jackson, Leona Mitchell and herself, Sarah Bazzell.[3]

In the 1947 handbook, the Methodist Youth Fellowship was described as "the coming together of the youth in the church for the purpose of solving some of the youth's problems in terms of cooperative effort." Fannie Johnson was president at that time, and she and the youth members were optimistic about the accomplishments of the coming year. It was the general feeling that they would be "more pronounced in every respect."[4]

Juanita Sharper, whose long time affiliation with Stewart Memorial afforded her opportunities to participate in many youth activities, recalled traveling to youth rallies. She remembered quite well the visit to Ebenezer UMC in Miami. Youths from churches throughout the state participated in such activities. Golden Smith and Mary Alice Smith also recalled their joyful experiences of working with the organization while attending Bethune-Cookman College.[5]

The Epworth League was replaced by the Methodist Youth Fellowship, which later became the United Methodist Youth Fellowship (UMYF). Leonard Tynes, Brenda Nicholson, Kim Thompson and Brent Davis were some of the active leaders of the organization.[6]

[2] Rev. Albert Emmanuel, *The Daytona Gazette-News*, April 13, 1901, 4.

[3] Mrs. Sarah B. Burns, "Historical Reflections," SMC 100th Anniversary Celebration.

[4] *Handbook of Stewart Memorial Methodist Church*, 1893 –1947, 7.

[5] Conversations with Mrs. J. Sharper, Dr. M. A. Smith and Rev. G. Smith.

[6] Church Bulletins: October 17, 1971; March 23, 1973; March 7, 1976.

During the 1970's the United Methodist Youth Fellowship was active, celebrating Youth Expression Day on October 31, 1971. The main speaker for this occasion was Calvin Williams, a young sophomore ministerial student at Bethune-Cookman College, who later became the pastor of Mount Zion A.M.E. Church of Daytona Beach. "Remember God in Thy Youth" was the title of his sermon. Brenda Nicholson, president of the UMYF, presided and several other youth members of Stewart Memorial participated, including: Wendy Thompson, Toni Gainey, Brenda Nicholson, Samuel Sharper, Jr., Theodore Nicholson, Jr., Leland Huger, Lynn Thompson, Stephen and Nathaniel Jenkins.[7]

Heading the UMYF in 1973 was Kim Thompson, who organized an ambitious program, utilizing skits, speakers and other creative activities. The youth group met the fourth Sunday of every month. The program announced for April 22 was one based on the Resurrection Story.[8]

Brent Davis, president of the United Methodist Youth Fellowship, and its sponsors: Barbara Blossom and Fannie Johnson were congratulated for the successful Youth Hour presented October 19, 1975.[9] Bringing the message for this occasion was Wayne Butler, a ministerial student at Bethune-Cookman College. With the assistance of Pinkie Bonaparte Oliver, Davis drafted an ambitious program for the spring and summer of 1976.[10]

Walter Granger, a junior from Bethune-Cookman College, was the main speaker for the special program of Sunday, July 17, 1977. Presiding over this activity was Brenda Nicholson. Other participants included Otis Kirksey, Wendy Thompson, and Stephen Jenkins and the Youth Choir.[11]

---

[7]Printed Program, October 31, 1971.

[8]Church Bulletin, March 25, 1973.

[9]Church Bulletin, October 26, 1975.

[10]Church Bulletin, March 7, 1976.

[11]Church Bulletin, July 17, 1977.

On November 20, 1977, Pastor Rogers P. Fair launched a week of youth activities at Stewart Memorial. On the 21st, he conducted a "Fellowship for Understanding Youth" for all youths and workers with youth programs at the church. Members of the Council on Ministries, the Deland Conference Youth Team and Stephen Jenkins, a guest consultant, assisted the Pastor. On Tuesday and Wednesday evening and on Sunday afternoon, periods of dedication and rededication for youths were held with Pinkie Bonaparte and Shirley Watts-Bing in charge. The activity climaxed with a musical ensemble from Deland performing.[12]

The youths enjoyed a variety of experiences in 1982. Younger Church Worship Services were held on the third Sunday from January to May. In addition, the youth ministry engaged in regular Bible study sessions. It also participated in such ventures as collecting money for UNICEF, and distributing Thanksgiving bags to the ill and recovering of Stewart Memorial. The Youth and Children Ministries also presented a pioneer appreciation luncheon for older members of the church, and they celebrated Christmas and Easter with special programs. Entertainment is important to the younger members of the church, and that was accomplished by such activities as pool parties and Christian Skate Nights. Since money is needed to perform worthwhile efforts, the Ministries sponsored a Spaghetti and Praise Supper as a fund raiser.[13]

The Youth and Children Ministries launched the 1983 year by worshipping at the Children's Home in Enterprise, FL. Members of these Ministries included Shirley Bing, Maxine Temple, Eileen Leonard, Celestine Demps Hinson, Fannie Rhodes, Gwendolyn Moore, Janet Jenkins, and Florence Roane. Sarah B. Burns was honored for her effort in preparing the Pioneer luncheon.[14]

---

[12]Church Bulletin, November 20, 1977.
[13]1982-83 Report for Youth and Children Ministries.
[14]Ibid.

The youths also were active in affairs of the Deland District. They participated in a January District Music Retreat in Leesburg, a March District Youth Council Meeting in Crescent City, a District Spring Rally in St. Augustine in May. In the latter activity, George Whitehead was elected District vice president and Eric Childs an alternate Youth Council representative. Two youths attended the School of Mission in Lakeland for honored graduates.[15]

Among the highlights of the 1984 year was the Afternoon of Music sponsored by the youths of Stewart on April 29. Among the youth choirs participating were Mt. Carmel Baptist, Mt. Bethel Institutional, Mt. Mission Baptist, Gray's Temple Church of God In Christ and the Greater Friendship Baptist.[16]

On March 18-19, 1985, a religious retreat was held at Stewart Memorial for the youths of the church. During this sleepover, these young people read and discussed sections of the Bible. Later that year, April 1, they took a trip to Lake Wales to see the traditional passion play.[17]

George I. Whitehead was the speaker for the youth program of June 12, 1988. Participating on that program also were Elaine Sharper, Ehrael Rivers, Geoffrey Sharper, Lawrence Temple, Jr., Tonjali Jenkin, Angela Demps, Adria Rhodes, Tracey Irvin and Ceronda Blevins.[18]

The summer, "Catch the Spirit Youth and Young Adult Revival" was applauded. Cooperating with this program was the First Union Bank, 130 Ridgewood Ave, which sponsored two $50.00 Saving Bonds to the most valuable player and runners up with good sportsmanship.[19]

On September 13, 1993, the youth Sunday School teachers joined the youths in the "Nite of Joy" Gospel Concerts at Walt

---

[15] Ibid.

[16] Church Bulletin, April 29, 1984.

[17] 1982-83 Report for Youth and Children Ministries.

[18] Church Bulletin, June 12, 1988.

[19] Church Bulletin, April 6, 1998.

Disney World.[20]

The Youth Ministry scheduled a trip to Atlanta for 19 youths and 15 adults. They visited historic Black colleges/universities, Martin Luther King Center for Nonviolence, and worshipped at Kelley Chapel. Kevin James, pastor, preached and the Youth Choir provided music.[21]

Through the years, the youth of Stewart Memorial have performed spiritual duties and helped to meet the financial needs of the church. Ms. Watts (Bing), the sponsor of the Youth Choir and youth activities was credited with encouraging the group to equip the pastor's study and provide a piano for the Fellowship Hall.[22]

[20] *SMUMC News*, August 1993.

[21] Church Bulletin, August 24, 1997.

[22] Interview with Ms. Watts (Bing).

Chapter 20

A Part of Methodism

> We can be effective as Christians if we are involved
> at all levels of the church. Problems that haunt us
> can be resolved if our time and resources are con-
> tributed generously.

Through the years, members of Stewart Memorial have been active on the district, state, jurisdictional, general and world levels. Those known to have participated are identified below.

Stewart Memorial as a Part of the Deland District

When Stewart Memorial became a part of the Florida Conference of the United Methodist Church in 1969, it was placed in the Deland District. As a member of that District, its members played active roles, and they continue to play essential roles in the East Central District in which the church was placed in 2006. Several members of Stewart Memorial were/are actively involved in the affairs of the District organizations.

Joel V. Fears, Sr. – Charge Lay Leader of Stewart Memorial, served in a similar role on the District level. He also served as president of the Deland District of the United Methodist Men. In addition he is serving/has served as a member of the following committees: Superintendency, Ministry, Leadership and

Lay Speaking. He also was a district trustee.[1] The District Board of Trustees is in charge of all property owned by the District.

James E. Huger – served as president of the Board. Likewise, he served as Director of Disaster Relief Preparedness, a member of the Board of Pensions, Preacher Relief Fund, the Board of Laity and Board on Superintendency.[2]

Sallie Shelton Culver – who served on several boards of the Florida Conference, also served as chair of the District Committee on Church and Society. Other committees of the Deland District in which she served or is serving include Worship, Nominations and Personnel, Lay Speaking Ministry (assistant to Ethel Grey, 1991-2005), Leadership, Disaster Recovery (1993-1996), Facilitator at District Training Events, and At-Large Delegate to Annual Conference.[3]

Others who have served or are serving on committees of the Deland District include: **Collace Greene**, Church Extension/ Building Committee;[4] **Charlie Long**, District Committee on Superintendency;[5] **John Heath**, Superintendency Committee;[6] and **Oswald P. Bronson**, the Board of Ministry.[7]

Several persons held offices in the District United Methodist Men and United Methodist Women, but they are discussed under those headings.

Stewart Memorial as a Part of the Florida Conference

To facilitate the smooth operation of the Florida Conference, local churches must supply it with well-qualified personnel. Stewart Memorial has met the challenge by making available several

---

[1] Program Calendar and Membership Directory, 1998, 2001, 2004.
[2] "Biography of Dr. James Huger," Men's Day Booklet, 2000.
[3] Memo from Mrs. Sallie Culver.
[4] Directory, 1998.
[5] Directory, 2004.
[6] 2001 Men's Day Celebration, 6.
[7] E.L. Wilks, *Chief Servant*, 177.

of its members for leadership roles in the Conference.

Richard V. Moore – who had been active with the Florida Conference of the Central Jurisdiction (CJ), was present on June 3, 1969, when it was consolidated with the Florida Conference (UMC).[8] After having served as lay leader of the Florida Conference (CJ) for several years, he was selected to serve as lay leader of the Florida Conference (UMC) for the 1972-1976 term.[9] In this role, he assumed responsibility for fostering "awareness of the role of the laity both within the congregation and through their ministries in the home, workplace, community and the world." Working with other officials of the church, he sought to enable and support "lay participation in the planning and decision-making process of the annual conference, district and local church.[10] Typical of his involvement in this role, he headed the Florida Delegation to the April 27, 1976 General Conference in Portland.[11]

Sallie Shelton Culver – answered the call to serve as chairperson of the Board of Trustees of the Florida United Methodist Children's Home in Enterprise, Florida 2001- 2005. That institution provides a Christian environment for children, who otherwise would have no true home environment. In its literature, it gives this description: "Through this Home, the influences of God's tender mercies and noble human compassion powerfully combine and intervene to lasting benefit, preserving and transforming," Culver had been a member of the Board of Trustees for five years prior to becoming its chairperson. In addition she served on several boards of the Florida Conference (UMC), including the Board of Ordained Ministry from 1996 to 2005. While on the Board, Culver worked on the Theology Team, Personal Growth Team, Elder Effectiveness Committee, Committee on Disability, Conference Relations Committee and Chair of an Interviewing Team. She also served on the Conference Com-

---

[8]*Florida Flame*, 350.

[9]Administrative Board, June 26, 1972.

[10]*Book of Discipline*, 603.9a.

[11]Administrative Board, March 29, 1976.

mittee on Church and Society and currently is a member of the Florida United Methodist Foundation since 2005.[12]

In 1996, the Council of Bishops called upon the United Methodist Church to reshape its life in response to the crisis among children and the impoverished and in faithfulness to Jesus Christ. In the 2001 Biblical and Theological Foundations document, the Bishops outlined goals for their initiative on Children and Poverty for 2001 – 2004.

Sheila Flemming – the former charge lay leader of Stewart Memorial, was asked to head the Florida Conference Bishop's Initiative on Children and Poverty.[13]

Mary Alice Smith – serves on the Board of Higher Education and Campus Ministry.[14] The Board seeks to develop Christian Disciples on Florida college campuses by encouraging them to develop personal relationship with Jesus Christ, and preparing them to be servant leaders. It is concerned with providing loans and scholarships for college students, as well as information concerning various opportunities.[15]

Theodore Jones (1972) – served on the Committee on Church Structures in Methodism.[16] As the denomination has grown and progressed, so has the local church, thus constructing new buildings is essential.

United Methodist Church General Conference

Attendance at the General Conference is a rare privilege. Mary McLeod Bethune, Richard V. Moore and Oswald P. Bronson have been delegates several times. Among the general conferences attended by Bethune were those in 1928 and the United Conference of 1939.[17] Moore attended the General and Ju-

---

[12]Memo from Mrs. Sallie Culver.

[13]Directory, 2001.

[14]Directory 2004.

[15]*Higher Education & Campus Ministry*, 2004, 18.

[16]Administrative Board, June 26, 1972.

[17]*Florida Flame.*

risdictional Conferences in 1956, 1960, 1964, 1972, 1976 and 1980.[18] Bronson was a delegate to the Jurisdictional and General Conference of the UMC in 1980, 1984, and 1988.[19] Among others who have attended the General Conference were Iona and Harry Burney, Jr., Rogers P. Fair and William Hayes. Records indicate that they were present at the 1972 General Conference in Atlanta.[20]

Stewart Memorial and World Methodism

Stewart Memorial has been active in world-wide Methodism. **Richard V.** and **B. J. Moore** were among those present at the World Conference on Methodism in London in 1966.[21] **Mary Alice Smith** also attended this global meeting. In addition, she attended the World Federation of Methodist Women in Wimbledon, England.[22]

Rogers P. Fair was one of 28 delegates from the Florida Conference to attend the 15th World Methodist Conference in Nairobi, Kenya in July-August, 1986. At this conference were delegates from 85 nations. The theme was "Christ Jesus: God's 'Yes' For the World."[23] On July 24 -31, 1991, Rogers and Agnes Fair attended the World Conference on Methodism in Singapore. The theme of that conference was "Jesus Christ God's Living Word."[24] Fair also has preached many sermons abroad. He delivered sermons at the historic Wesley Church in Oxford, England in 1959, 1965 and he preached there on July 29, 1973.[25] Fair also was a member of the American Methodist delegation to study "Basis for World Peace" in 1964. On his vis-

---

[18] A Birthday Celebration in Honor of Dr. Richard V. Moore, November 17, 1991.
[19] Wilks, 178.
[20] Administrative Board, June 26, 1972.
[21] Homegoing Celebration of Dr. Richard V. Moore, Sr. January 8, 1994.
[22] Resume of Dr. Mary Alice Smith.
[23] *SMUMC News*, September 1986.
[24] Celebration, March 14, 1993.
[25] Church Bulletin, July 15, 1973.

its abroad in 1984-85, he was chosen by the United Methodist delegation to preach in the Soviet Union, Poland and South Korea.[26]

Dr. Oswald Bronson undertook a study of conditions in Haiti for the Board of Global Ministries of the United Methodist Church.[27]

---

[26]Celebration, March 14, 1993.
[27]Wilks, 178.

Chapter 21

Bethune-Cookman College (University)

Although separate, they have a purpose in common,
And that purpose is to glorify the Lord.
Each in a unique way, its function will perform,
As they work together in one accord.
Each to humanity is obligated for service,
And each to the other, some service can give.
Because each helps the other, a better role to play
The impact on humanity for many years will live.

When Rogers P. Fair assumed the pastoral charge at Stewart Memorial, he also began his teaching career at Bethune-Cookman College. Thus he perceived a good relation between the two institutions. The 1947 Stewart Memorial Handbook reads:

Ranking among our foremost Methodist Colleges, Bethune-Cookman College and Stewart Memorial maintain a functional relationship in points of service to each other and a sympathetic understanding of a common outlook. Bethune-Cookman's students and faculty find a continuity of purpose in Stewart Memorial; likewise, Stewart Memorial finds the same in Bethune-Cookman; they both point the way toward better living through

Christ. Hundreds of students and many faculty members worship at Stewart Memorial from week to week. In fact, the president, Richard V. Moore, is a sincere, hard working churchman.[1]

A close relation always existed between Bethune-Cookman College and Stewart Memorial. Early in Mary McLeod Bethune's efforts to build an educational institution, Stewart Memorial played a pivotal role. Her students often appeared there in concerts or as a part of the services in money-raising efforts. The church also was the meeting place of Bethune and her students with two men of wealth: James Gamble and George Doane. Her guests were impressed with the plans she outlined for her school and supported it financially.[2]

Later, Mary McLeod Bethune became a trustee of Stewart Memorial, and in that role aided the church in obtaining needed funds. In 1926, she became a co-signer for a bank loan.[3] Her early leadership in the church was followed by later presidents of Bethune-Cookman College. Richard V. Moore served as charge lay leader of the church, and he held several other major offices, including chairman of the Building Committee. Both Oswald Bronson and Trudie Kibbe-Reed held/hold membership in Stewart Memorial while serving as president of the College.[4] Dr. Texas A. Adams, college physician and long time trustee, served simultaneously in several key positions at Stewart Memorial.[5] The same was/is true with many of the other college officials.

Jerome F. Del Pino, Rogers P. Fair, Kevin James, and Michael Frazier, all served simultaneously as director of religious services or chaplain of Bethune-Cookman College, and pastor of Stewart Memorial.[6] Acting in dual roles, they were

[1] *Handbook of Stewart Memorial Methodist Church, 1893 -1947,* 4.
[2] Nancy Ann Zrinyi Long, *The Life and Legacy of Mary McLeod Bethune* (Cocoa, FL: Florida Historical Society, 2004), 12-13.
[3] Merchants Bank and Trust Company, Bank Note, June 1, 1926.
[4] Membership Roster.
[5] See Appendix.
[6] Ibid.

in excellent positions to facilitate college-church cooperation. Arthur Crowell, Carrill Munnings, Joreatha Capers, Walter Monroe and others also taught classes at the college while serving as pastor.[7]

Even when pastors were not working at Bethune-Cookman College, they had good relations with it because of their alumni standing. While it is difficult to ascertain how many pastors fall in that category, of recent pastors, we can identify William Higgins, Alfonso Delaney, Kevin James, Michael Frazier and Walter Monroe as graduates of Bethune-Cookman College.[8]

Professors, administrators, staff members, and alumni compose most of the adult membership of Stewart Memorial. This environment assures a positive relation between the church and college.

Dating back as long as could be remembered the freshmen and new students have worshipped with the Stewart Memorial family at the beginning of the academic year. Traditionally, the students have come to the church, but some recent services have been held on the campus because of better accommodations. There have been occasions when the church has been invited to worship as a group at the college. In August 1971, the church was invited to worship at the Contemporary Celebration of the Holy Communion,[9] and on January 3, 1972 permission was granted by the Administrative Council for the membership of Stewart Memorial to worship at Bethune-Cookman College during the Easter services. The other guests were the 400 or more members of the United Beauty School Owners and Teachers Association.[10]

Stewart Memorial has been a fertile field for the training of young ministers. Ministerial students of Bethune-Cookman found it to be a convenient location to launch their careers. The work Oswald Bronson did at Stewart Memorial under Rogers P.

---

[7]Ibid.

[8]Ibid.

[9]Administrative Board, August 31, 1971.

[10]Administrative Board, January 1, 1972.

Fair during the late forties convinced him to make a change from the Church of God to Methodism. While a student at Bethune-Cookman, he read the Scripture, delivered prayers and delivered sermons at Stewart Memorial. He was one of many ministerial students who expressed appreciation for the valuable Stewart Memorial experience.[11] Alfonso Delaney also recalled having a rich experience as Pastor Rogers Fair's assistant at the church, while studying at Bethune-Cookman College.[12]

While students have gained from their experiences with Stewart Memorial, they have been instrumental in helping the church to fulfill its mission. Calvin Williams, a longtime pastor of Mount Zion A.M.E. Church of the city, availed himself of services at Stewart Memorial on several occasions, while a student at Bethune-Cookman. Illustrative of this was his sermon delivered on October 31, 1971, for Youth Expression Day.[13] Wayne Butler, a ministerial student, also was helpful in promoting the youth ministry. He was the main speaker for the Youth Hour of October 19, 1975.[14] Walter Granger, a junior from the college, was the main speaker for the special program of Sunday, July 17, 1977.[15] Through the years, Stewart Memorial has continued the practice of being a valuable pulpit for student ministers. Kevin James and Michael Frazier both served in ministerial roles at the church while students. David Allen, now a pastor in St. Petersburg, was an active ministerial student. Not only did he deliver sermons, but he availed himself of services with the Growth and Enrichment Ministry and with programs related to young adults.[16]

Initiated during the pastoral charge of Joreatha McCall Capers were activities on the campus to welcome new students and

---

[11]E. L. Wilks, *Chief Servant, Legacies and Memories* (2004), 32.

[12]Letter from Dr. Alfonso Delaney.

[13]Church Bulletin, October 31, 1971.

[14]Church Bulletin, March 7, 1976.

[15]Church Bulletin, July 15, 1977.

[16]Letter of Thanks to Minister David Allen from Growth and Enrichment Ministry, November 24, 1997; *SMUMC, The Vine*, December 1997.

their parents to Bethune-Cookman. The B-CC Welcome Booth, which was under the Events Ministry, but presently organized by the Higher Education and Campus Ministry Committee, has drawn much praise from parents of new students. Mary Alice Smith is chair of this committee.[17]

Through the years, pastors have sought to develop programs that reached out to Bethune-Cookman's students. Michael Frazier, in defending the "Hour of Power" services commented:

> The vision for this service is to reach out to the college community and provide students with a unique worship encounter that speaks to their needs. Moreover, this service creates a spiritual environment where the students can feel free to exercise their gifts and graces for ministry.[18]

Walter E. Monroe listed as one of his three major goals "to affirm and support the historical relationship between Stewart Memorial United Methodist Church and Bethune-Cookman College." His vision statement was "Where Christ, Campus and Community Meet to Grow in Christ."[19] Typical of college-church relations was the participation of Bethune-Cookman College's faculty members in the services on World Communion Day and during the celebration of Pentecost.[20] Thursday evening Bible class for students of Bethune-Cookman College was another outreach program designed to better church-college relations. The class is taught by Sedrick Harris.[21]

Joreatha Capers recalled the cooperation that existed between the church and the college during her tenure as pastor. On June 14-16, 1996, the Women of Stewart Memorial and Bethune-Cookman College Urban Outreach hosted the first National Women's Inner Healing Conference, "Advance '96 - An

---

[17]Church Bulletin, September 3, 2006.

[18]Charge Conference Report, 1993.

[19]Charge Conference Report, 2005.

[20]Church Bulletin, June 4, 2006.

[21]Church Bulletin, October 8, 2006.

Inner Healing Convocation: The Journey to Wholeness; Woman to Woman Ministries, Inc."[22]

Students also play a vital role in the music program at the church. The present music coordinator, Kevin Cooper, is the assistant director of the Bethune-Cookman Concert Chorale. Also this cooperation is made easier since Rebecca Steel, the director of the College's Concert Chorale, is also a member of Stewart Memorial. One of the College's musical groups is almost always available for special occasions at the church.[23]

Stewart Memorial has been generous in opening its doors to affairs at the College, which could not be accommodated on the campus at the time. The Model United Nations launched its first conference at the church in 1979,[24] and when Heyn Memorial Chapel was being repaired, certain events, including the opera workshop, were held at Stewart Memorial. Following the series of rehearsals, the Bethune-Cookman College Opera Workshop and Chamber Singers presented one of their "Music Around the World" concerts at the church.[25] Likewise, the auditorium and dining hall of Bethune-Cookman College have been used to accommodate events which could not be held at the church.

The relationship between Bethune-Cookman College and Stewart Memorial has been one of mutual hospitality.

[22]Memo from Dr. Joreatha Capers.
[23]Church Bulletins and Observations.
[24]Model United Nations History.
[25]Bethune-Cookman College, Opera Workshop and Chamber Singers' "Music Around the World" April 13, 1999, Souvenir Program.

Chapter 22

The Ecumenical Community

Since all churches profess a belief in God,
A common cause they should seek to advance.
Through working together, each can achieve its goal,
To glorify God, and His purpose enhance.

To work cooperatively with other churches has been a goal of Stewart Memorial from the outset. At the time of its founding, it worked effectively with other Black churches in the community: Mount Bethel Baptist Institutional Church and Mt. Zion A.M.E. Articles in the Daytona Gazette News indicate that pastors of the various Black churches cooperated in their services, especially rallies. Unfortunately, however, segregated practices of that day limited Stewart Memorial's interaction with White Methodist churches in the area. A retired White Methodist minister, however, gave a contribution that enabled the members of the struggling church to erect a permanent building.

As Stewart Memorial grew, so did the African-American Christian community; thus, there were many opportunities for cooperation among churches. Some of these interactions were with inter-church alliances and some were with individual

155

churches. Ministers of Stewart Memorial have affiliated with different ministerial organizations and have pursued various ecumenical projects. Rogers P. Fair was a charter member of the Halifax Ministerial Association in 1956, and later became president of the interracial organizations.[1] The association presented many ecumenical activities. Pastors of Stewart Memorial also participated, then and now, in other area ministerial alliances, including the current Daytona Black Clergy Alliance.

Since more than one church is involved in promoting God's causes here on earth, every church should seek to promote Christian unity. Each church should work cooperatively in resolving matters of inter-religious concern. Records of earlier years are not available, but by the late sixties, Stewart Memorial had in existence an ecumenical committee, which sought to enhance cooperation among churches. In 1970, the committee worked with individuals of other churches in canvassing the community in search of persons who had no church affiliation. They sought to direct such individuals to churches of their choices. At that time, Margaret Gibbs chaired the committee.[2]

Historically, Stewart Memorial has worked with other churches in its effort to communicate useful information to the African-American community. Typical of this was the effort to secure representatives from other churches for a meeting at Stewart Memorial on November 8, 1973, to be informed of a program scheduled to become effective on January 1, 1974, on supplemental benefits for persons over 65, blind and disabled.[3]

There are many events, which can be more effective when pursued by several churches, and on many occasions, Stewart Memorial has joined with others in sponsoring such ecumenical activities. Emancipation Day, which for years was a major celebration for African Americans, was one of such events. Typical

---

[1]Leonard Lempel, "Reverend Rogers P. Fair: A Champion of Racial Equality and Interracial Harmony," Vol. 24, No. 24 (Summer 2006), 2-5.

[2]Administrative Board, April 27, 1970.

[3]Administrative Board, October 29, 1973.

of such New Year's Day services was the one held in 1962 at
Stewart Memorial. Henry Tanner, pastor of St. Johns Baptist
Church (Ormond) was the main speaker for the occasion. Music
was provided by choirs from New Bethel A. M. E. (Ormond),
Mount Bethel Baptist Institutional, New Mount Zion Baptist,
and Allen Chapel A. M. E. Presiding over the gathering was Eugene Tillman of Mt. Bethel. Other participating ministers were
the pastors of Morning Star Baptist, New Bethel, New Mount
Zion, Allen Chapel and the chaplain of Bethune-Cookman College. J. H. Adams, pastor of Stewart Memorial was the host
minister.[4]

Perhaps replacing Emancipation Day in importance among
African American churches is the Martin Luther King's Day
Prayer Breakfast, sponsored by area ministers. Stewart Memorial has been a long-time participant in this event, which is open
to the public.

Easter services also have afforded Stewart Memorial opportunities to participate in ecumenical activities. One of the more
impressive area-wide Easter Sunrise services was held on April
2, 1972, at the band shell on the beach. The Halifax Area Ministerial Association sponsored the services. Shirley Watts Bing of
Stewart Memorial served as pianist for the occasion.[5] For many
years, this was an annual affair for Stewart Memorial. Also
memorable was the sunrise service held at the Ocean Center in
1991. Pastor Alfonso Delaney presided and ushers served for
the occasion.[6]

In addition to the sunrise services, sponsored by the Halifax
Ministerial Association, Stewart Memorial has joined with individual churches in Easter celebrations. Rogers P. Fair preached
at the Good Friday Service at St. Timothy's Episcopal in 1976.
The Stewart Memorial family joined him.[7] The Good Friday

[4]"Emancipation Proclamation Observance" *The Stewart Memorial Herald*, January 1962.
[5]Church Bulletin, March 26, 1972.
[6]"Recapping Holy Week," *Stewart Memorial UMC News*, April 1991.
[7]Church Bulletin, April 11, 1976.

services for 1991 were held at First United Methodist Church
with Alfonso Delaney delivering the message and twelve choir
members of Stewart Memorial were participants in the choir for
the day.[8] Carrill Munnings recalled leading community pastors
in a combined 3-hour Good Friday Noon Worship service of
Drama and Preaching from the Seven Last Words of Jesus, during his tenure at Stewart Memorial. During the tenure of Joreatha Capers there were many cooperative efforts with Tubman
King U.C.C., Allen Chapel A.M.E. and the Greater Friendship
Baptist Church , especially at Easter for Seven (7) Last Words
and/or Easter Sunrise Service in Daisy Stocking Park.[9]

Thanksgiving services also have been occasions when
churches interacted as an ecumenical group. Typical of such a
service was that of Thanksgiving 1977, which was sponsored
by the Halifax Area Ministerial Association. On that occasion,
Robert Smith, the pastor of the First Presbyterian Church,
delivered the sermon, and the Stewart Memorial Combined
Choirs and ushers served.[10]

Stewart Memorial has participated with Allen Chapel in presenting several Christmas productions. Carrill Munnings applauded the decision of the two churches to present the program
twice in 1992, once at each church. Charles Long of Stewart
and Barbara Bouie of Allen directed the presentations, jointly.
Although the program was a presentation of the two churches,
participation was open to participants of all churches. The program was dedicated to Carrill Munnings and Michael Bouie of
Allen Chapel, both new ministers at their respective churches.[11]

Stewart Memorial has also participated in the activities of
the "World Day of Prayer," an event usually held at the International Speedway. But the 2006 World Day of Prayer was held
at the Mary McLeod Bethune Performing Arts Center.

Virtually every ministry of Stewart Memorial has pursued

---

[8]*SMUMC News*, April 1991.

[9]E-mails from Rev. C. S. Munnings and Dr. Joreatha Capers.

[10]Church Bulletin, November 20, 1977.

[11]*SMUMC News*, November 1992.

joint efforts with other churches. Among those pursuing ecumenical efforts were the Music Ministry, ushers and Church
School. Historic records indicate that the Men's Interdenominational Choir participated on the Men's Night program of the
44th anniversary celebration of Stewart Memorial in 1937,[12]
and musical groups of Stewart Memorial have made appear-
ances at other churches, especially when their ministers were
delivering sermons. The annual Christmas cantata, under the direction of Lucian and Olive Lewis, always included musicians
from other churches, and appealed to an ecumenical audience.
Later, Stewart Memorial joined with Allen A.M.E. Church to
continue the Christmas cantata.[13]

Ushers of Stewart Memorial are affiliated with the city-wide
Ushers Union—an organization made up of ushers from various churches in the area. Meetings rotate among the member
churches. For special occasions at member churches, ushers
from Stewart Memorial usually are asked to serve. The favor is
returned when Stewart Memorial hosts special events.[14]

The Disciple Bible Class was an innovative program that
attracted interested Bible students from other churches. There
were nine graduates in the 1997-98, including four members
from other churches: Bernita Bobo and Nettie Ryan from New
Mount Zion Baptist Church, Essie Robinson from Shiloh Baptist, and Edna Fields of the First Assembly of God. Olivia Durant and Jean Prosser from Highland Presbyterian Church and
Jimmie Rhinehart of New Mount Zion participated in earlier
programs.[15]

Through the years, Vacation Bible School has utilized a variety of formats: an individual church project, a bi-church program, and a multi-church project. In 2005 and 2006, Stewart Memorial participated in community-wide vacation Bible

---

[12]Celebration of the Forty-Fourth Anniversary of Stewart Memorial
Methodist Episcopal Church, Souvenir Program, December 15-19, 1937.

[13]SMUMC News, November 1992.

[14]Memo from Mrs. Eloise Snell.

[15]The Vine, June 1998.

Schools sponsored by the Daytona Black Clergy Alliance.[16]
Other churches which participated in these programs were Allen
Chapel A.M.E., Divine Deliverance, Greater Friendship Baptist, Mt. Carmel Baptist, New St. James Baptist, Tubman King
Church of Christ, and Shiloh Baptist.[17] Prior to the inception of
this program, Stewart Memorial had a Vacation Bible School ar-
rangement with Shiloh Baptist, with the school alternating from
year to year.[18] During the period of the early eighties, Stewart Memorial, under an agreement negotiated by Sallie Shelton Culver, conducted a unified vacation Bible school with First
Methodist Church.[19]

On February 21, 1993, members of First United Methodist
of Ormond Beach joined with members of SMUMC in a collo-
quy on "Racism and Prejudice" as "diseases that endanger our
spiritual lives." Among the participants were Joseph Ampiaw,
Mary Alice Smith and Jake Miller from SMUMC and Bill Beck
and Donna Brandymeyer from First United. Cleo Higgins and
Mary Beck, directors of Christian education in their respective
churches, led the dialogue with the audience. Following the discussion, Thurman Stanback directed a five-person reader's the-
ater in a presentation of "Black Voices from Slavery through
the Present." Participating in this presentation were Amelia
Colston, Juanita Sharper, Lawrence Temple, Cleo Higgins and
Thurman Stanback. The affair was followed by a dinner hosted
by Phannye Huger and the SMUMC hospitality staff.[20]

On Nov 13, 1993, Stewart Memorial and Community
United Methodist sponsored jointly the "Rainbow" City-wide
Golf Tournament.[21]

At its Second Honors Banquet, Stewart Memorial extended
an invitation for other churches to honor outstanding members

---

[16]Church Bulletins: July 10, 2005 and July 16, 2006.
[17]Church Bulletin, June 4, 2006.
[18]Information provided by Mrs. Childs.
[19]Memo from Mrs. Sallie Shelton Culver.
[20]*SMUMC News*, March 1993, Vol. 3, No. 3.
[21]*SMUMC News*, October 1993 , Vol. 3, No. 10.

from their congregations. Among those honored were: Bennie Tooley, Greater Friendship Baptist; Patricia Jones, Mt. Carmel Missionary Baptist; Gertrude Smith, St. Timothy's Episcopal; Henry Oliver, Mt. Zion A.M.E.; Ruth Hankerson, New St. James Baptist; and Johnny MacDonald, Shady Grove Baptist.[22]

The Third Honors Banquet honored these persons from community churches: Thelma Alderman, St Timothy Episcopal Church; Valetta Butler, Greater Friendship Baptist Church; Ruth Hankerson, New St. James; Carolyn Johnson, Hope Fellowship; Dorothy Thomas, Shiloh Missionary Baptist Church and Shirley A. White, New Mt. Zion Baptist Church.[23]

Through the years, Stewart Memorial and its pastors have done much to enhance the ecumenical efforts, and, thus, have helped to establish the concept of *one church.*

---

[22] Second Honors Banquet, February 28, 1997 (Printed Program).

[23] Honors Banquet February 26, 1998 (Printed Program).

Chapter 23

The Local Community

Cooperation should exist between church and community
Since each on the other so often must depend
If together they work, common enemies to destroy,
Poverty, violence and greed can come to an end.

Stewart Memorial has played an active role in the community, both the church at large and its individual members. When Thomas Walker, the founding pastor, came to Daytona Beach in 1893 there were few African Americans who had education on his level. He was a teacher and preacher, and because of his skills in carpentry, he could provide many services which many members of the Black community could not provide for themselves.[1] Later ministers also were skillful and made use of their skills in helping to build the Daytona community, which was in the emerging stage. When Albert Emanuel came to the city to assume the pastoral charge in 1901, he helped to keep the people informed concerning happenings in the city through his column in the *Daytona Gazette*. Articles indicated that he visited such institutions as the kindergarten, which was recently started. He expressed gratitude to those who had made this early form of education possible, and he urged the people to utilize

---

[1]Biography of Thomas H. B. Walker, Appendix.

this educational program.[2] Emanuel also used his pen to challenge African Americans of the Daytona area, "do not spend all your money riding on excursions but give us a dollar to fix the street." In supporting the call for a proposed meeting to consider the problem of inadequate streets, he wrote:

> The people of Midway are very anxious to have Palm Street extended to the railroad and down to the depot. In our present condition we are put to much inconvenience. Those who come from the south part of town must go all the way down Ridgewood to Second Avenue, nearly a mile out of the way, or to prevent this long walk they come down Volusia Avenue to the depot and then go about 400 yards up the railroad track, which is very dangerous for our wives and children. . . .[3]

Because of the scarcity of public meeting places at that time, the Stewart Chapel was available for such meetings. To this present day, the sanctuary and fellowship hall of Stewart Memorial continue to be used for public meetings, family reunions, fraternity and sorority activities and other functions.[4]

Stewart Memorial has supported many civic organizations of the community. For years, it has been a life member of the National Association for the Advancement of Colored People and is a supporter of its regular activities. As pastor, Rogers P. Fair was strongly supportive of the NAACP, and urged the congregation to be likewise. According to him:

> There is no better organization than the NAACP to lead us into the real battle for equality. We have a thousand problems, and must begin to chip away at

---

[2] *Daytona Gazette.*
[3] See Trustee Reports.
[4] *Daytona Times*, March 7 -13, 1979.

them in a hurry.[5]

For years, Charles W. Cherry, Sr., a member of Stewart Memorial, headed the local branch and state chapter, and served on the national Board of Directors. At the time of this writing (2006), Joel Fears, Sr. serves as vice president of the Volusia County – Daytona Beach Branch.[6]

Stewart Memorial also has been a strong supporter of the efforts of the Friends of the John H. Dickerson Heritage Library, sponsoring a table at its annual Author's Luncheon, since its inception. Several members of Stewart Memorial are on the board of the Friends organization.[7]

Through the years, the church has supported the Richard V. Moore Center and the Westside Business and Professional Organization. Many members of Stewart Memorial have been affiliated with both organizations. Charles Cherry was instrumental in organizing the first, and Rogers P. Fair chaired it. Richard V. Moore was actively involved in both.[8] The church also has been supportive of the Habitat for Humanity and similar projects.[9]

Through the years, it has sought to communicate with the larger community through radio, television, and newspaper. Typical of such programs was the 1947-1948 thirty minute radio program featuring Rogers P. Fair, which was sponsored by the Herbert Thompson Funeral Home.[10] He also wrote a weekly column for the *Daytona Times* during its early years.[11] During the pastoral charge of Michael Frazier and Eddie J. Rivers, Stewart Memorial sponsored a one-hour radio program

---

[5]Biography of Charles Cherry in "Men's Day Booklet, and Listing of Officers," 2006.

[6]Author's Luncheon Programs.

[7]Funeral Program of Dr. Richard V. Moore, January 8, 1994.

[8]Program Calendar and Membership Directory, 2004, 1.

[9]Notes from Mrs. Agnes Fair.

[10]*Daytona Times*, 1979 editions.

[11]Author's recollections.

of regular church services.[12] Rev. Alfonso Delaney participated in the Daily Devotion Program for WESH, Television Channel 2. He participated in the daily Sign-On and Sign-Off programs of 1991 on: July 14, July 15, Sept 4, Oct 13, Oct 14, Nov 3, and Nov 4.

Stewart Memorial has a history of seeking to advance the community through its regular programs. Scouting is perhaps the best example. Although there are few participants in the program from Stewart Memorial, the church sees an advantage in supporting such community-related programs.

The Girl Scouts can be traced back to at least 1945, when Margaret Bartley headed the program. It was described as an ally to the church since "it stresses principles and morals that are conducive to good living and character development." [13] The Boy Scouts program also has its roots deep in history. The Anthony M. Stephens Boy Scout Troop # 108, named in honor of a long time scout advocate and former committeeman, is more than fifty years old. Through the years, it has had such dedicated leaders as William A. McMillan, former academic dean of Bethune-Cookman College; Charles Cherry, civil rights leader; Neil Crosslin, local physician; and Joel Fears, Sr., Willie Scott, William Bell and Hayward Evans, Sr. [14] According to the announcement, "Camping and hiking experiences are usually provided monthly with an opportunity for scouts to get close to nature and put into practice many of the things learned during weekly meetings."[15]

Scout Troop 108, which is under the sponsorship of the United Methodist Men, also receives support from the Beta Delta Lambda Chapter of Alpha Phi Alpha Fraternity, Inc.[16]

Being cognizant of the need to improve the performances of minority students in the school system, Stewart Memo-

---

[12]*SMUMC News*, July 1991, 8.

[13]*SMUMC News*, October 1993.

[14]Ibid.

[15]UMM Minutes, September 20, 2003.

[16]*SMUMC News,* August 2002.

rial initiated and supported programs designed to meet that need. One of such programs was the Jump Start Program in 2000-2002, which was made possible by a grant secured from the Deland District of the United Methodist Women of the United Methodist Church, and supported with additional financial support from Stewart Memorial. Under the provisions of the grant, twenty students from Bonner Elementary School participated in a five-day per week after-school program, in which they completed their homework, were tutored in reading and mathematics, and were given individual and small group assistance. During the program, they were exposed to Christian values. Other benefits of the program were that they were given healthy snacks, as well as provided recreational activities. Locally, those who spearheaded the program were Lay Leader Sheila Flemming and Outreach Chairman Jessie Childs, who wrote the proposal.[17]

Many of the programs of the church are designed to provide information to the general public. Illustrative of these are political and health forums which usually are held in conjunction with Men and Women's Day activities.[18]

The annual Christmas cantatas, which were conducted for several years, beginning in 1981, had vast community appeal. Although under the direction of Stewart Memorial, participants were always from several churches.[19] Likewise, the free presentation was a Christmas event, which the community looked forward to attending.

Pastor Joreatha Capers recalled her efforts to take the church out of its four-walls sanctuary into the community. Praise and worship services were held in the Joe Harris Park.

Taking the church into the community is a major goal of Stewart Memorial. Its Mission Statement reads:

The mission and ministry of this church is to be a

---

[17]Men and Women's Day Booklets.

[18]Author's recollections.

[19]Printed Programs of Cantata.

concerned, faithful, and caring community reaching out to all. It is the purpose of each witness herein to disperse God's love and gospel throughout our community in Christian activities as well as through daily living.

Chapter 24

Pastoral Remarks

In the United Methodist Church, pastors serve for a designated period and then move on to other callings. Some leave behind them powerful messages which could by word of mouth be passed on to later generations, but most of their sermons are forgotten shortly after they are delivered. Fortunately, most of the sermons of the recent pastors are recorded for posterity. Some of the pastors left printed words that can be found in newsletters of the church. It may be of interest to review copies of the pastors' words as they appeared in the *Stewart-Memorial Herald*, *Stewart Memorial United Methodist Church News (SMUMC)*, *The Vine*, and the *Good News Journal*. When spiritual advice is given in writing, it can be read time and again and the second or third reading may be more meaningful.

Early in his ministry at Stewart Memorial, Rogers P. Fair wrote these words which are as meaningful today as they were when he penned them. He wrote:

> In days like these the church must organize to survive. Her evangelistic program can no longer depend upon the traditional "August Revival." The beginning of every day must see some new task begun, while the close of each day must see some

progress made.[1]

Fair challenged Christians to be active and reject "passive religion." According to the incoming pastor, Christianity must be reflected in whatever we do.

In 1986, Eddie J. Rivers expressed a similar concern in regard to "living the life of a Christian." In addressing the problem of church and sin, he issued this challenge:

> When known sin in the church goes unchecked, other believers feel greater freedom to venture into unrighteousness. The church becomes weak and ineffective. Its power for life and ministry disappears.[2]

In his remarks, he warned the congregation that the failure of churches to "deal with known sin" has caused them to lose their role as a "powerful, credible witness in their communities." On the other hand, he suggested, "When churches do address their sin, the community takes notice." He reminded the church of the Biblical statement, "Let your light so shine before men, that they may see your good works, and glorify your Father which is in heaven"(Matt 5:16).

Alfonso Delaney saw great benefits gained from reading the Bible on a regular schedule. He offered this advice:

> The Bible is a sure guide for living and for bearing witness to the supremacy of God. When we read about those long ago Biblical figures in the Bible, we learn that they were people just like you and me, and the help they got from God is just as available to us as it was to them. We all at some time or other wonder, "what is life all about?" "What is my purpose for being here?" "How can I solve this problem that is a constant thorn in the side?" Whether

---

[1] *Handbook of Stewart Memorial Methodist Church, 1893 –1947.*
[2] *SMUMC News* (Rivers), September 1986.

the trouble we need help with is sickness, sin, jeal-
ousy, hatred, discordant relationship, or something
else, you are guaranteed to find all of the answers
to these questions in the Bible. In my own personal experience in search to understand God and
my purpose of being, God speaks to me through his
Divine Word in the Holy Bible.[3]

During Carrill Munnings's pastorate, he appealed to fellow
Christians for constant prayer. He was especially concerned
with giving praise to God for His many acts of goodness. He
wrote:

Despite all of the tumultuous experiences and moments of conflagration in our lives, we ought to
praise him...For he has seen us through; he has
been our guide. God has been our ground of hope,
and he has sustained us.[4]

He reminded us that our ancestors praised God, even during time of slavery, and according to Munnings, God sustained
them. Referring to Psalm 150: 1-2, he advised us that:

...We ought to praise God because of God's
mighty deeds. The Lord has moved his hand so
mightily in the lives of so many of us! We do
not stand in the positions that many of us enjoy
standing in today all because of ourselves. So we
really ought to praise him![5]

Also of major concern to Munnings were the youths of our
church and the community in which they live. Noting that "none
of us is safe, if the young person is not safe." He called upon the

---

[3] *SMUMC News* (Delaney), February 1992.
[4] *SMUMC News* (Munnings) October 1993.
[5] Ibid.

Stewart Memorial congregation to "prayerfully work together to support our work of ministry toward our young people." He made the following observation:

> Rarely, do we stop to realize the great blessings that the Lord has given us "in safety!" Some of us like to think that we can rely on bars, alarms, guns, locks, dogs, security monitoring services, etc.: but God gives us safety indeed!

> As my father once told me, "Locks keep honest people out! We need not ever forget that the expert thief breaks in where and when he or she wants. The things mentioned above do provide us a measure of safety and security; but they don't guarantee safety. Truly, safety is granted through the grace of God. This is especially true with spiritual safety!

> Jesus said, "the thief comes to steal, kill and destroy, but I have come that they might have life abundantly" (John 10:10) Many are those people who claim to have get rich schemes which will provide the good life in America. However, only Christ delivers abundant life (and satisfying life) from the source—a personal relationship with God![6]

Rogers Fair has written about the woes of the family on several occasions. Noting that, "the shape of the future will greatly depend upon the teaching of today," He selected to write these words to an audience beyond Stewart Memorial:

> As teachers and preachers and other youth-related professionals, we have the tools with which to mold and remold the human clay that sometimes appears shapeless and hopeless.

---

[6]*SMUMC News*, August 1993.

We can seek to give youth something that has been vital in all periods of history.

First and foremost, we can give to the youth of our day a **sense of direction**. A lack of direction is often the problem with young people who appear indifferent and wayward. Many youths simply are not certain of who they are or where they are going.[7]

In May 1995, Joreatha Capers directed her attention and the congregation to the importance of the family as Stewart Memorial celebrated National Family Month. She wrote:

The family circle and our circle of friends form two of the most important circles in our lives. It is within these circles that we should receive nurture inspiration, enlightenment, encouragement, coping skills, as well as first hand experience in the knowledge of what it means to be in relationship with other human beings. Yes, not only are we "what we eat," but to a large degree, we are also a "product of our environment." We have heard such quotes from the Bible as, "Train up a child in the way he should go, and when he is old he will not turn from it." (Proverbs 22:6)

That is why it is so important for a family to have God at the center of the circle. Equally important to our lives is the spiritual family... the community of believers... the church. It must provide needed guidance, support and reinforcement for the work begun by the biological family. All of this helps the church to live out its calling to the world, and aids in the up building of God's kingdom.[8]

---

[7] *Daytona Times*, February 7 -12, 1979.

[8] Dr. Joreatha McCall Capers, Annual Women's Day Observance May 28, 1995.

Also focusing on the importance of the family, Fair perceived its failure to be a major cause of the problems of youth. To him, "the rigid rise in the divorce rate and family separation without divorce had many disastrous affects." These family problems combined with other problems to make the burdens of youth almost unbearable. He observed:

> Our youth, the weight of these problems is much too great to be born by split families. To bring this fact closer to home, we are aware of the fact ... at a time when we are plagued with a multitude of social problems among that, even with both the mother and father image in the home, the bringing up of a family in times like these is a tremendous task. The growth of the drug culture, the almost unlimited use of alcohol, both at home and in the community, the free and open practice of sex, plus the situational pressures that affect both young and old, separate today's family from that of yesterday's family. And added to this is the peer pressure under which our young people must labor to be recognized, making a stable family all the more necessary in times like these.[9]

Christmas is a meaningful time to challenge the congregation. Often Christmas has to be defined for them. Kevin James in his sermon in writing in December 1997, wrote:

> It is during the celebration of the birth of Jesus Christ that we worship, love, and serve God, who promises always to come and bless us with forgiveness and unmerited love. This is a great opportunity for members, friends, co-workers or parishioners to reaffirm their love, faith and commitment to Jesus Christ our Savior who is a perfect gift from

---

[9] *Daytona Times*, April 19-25, 1979.

God. "For God so loved the world that he gave his only begotten Son that whosoever believeth in him should not perish, but have everlasting life."(John 3:16) Through His Son, the divine Logos, we have eternal life, eternal joy, and eternal peace. Jesus Christ is the undisputed perfect Gift given to humankind.

Personally, Christmas is not exchanging gifts as pleasantries to my family and friends only. It is my opportunity to celebrate through worship, to serve and love the most priceless, charitable and an unselfish gift of all time during this holiday season, as a gift to our Savior and King, Jesus Christ.[10]

In a challenge to women of Stewart Memorial, Michael Frazier penned these words:

Continue to be as vigilant as you have been in the past! Stay on the path... giving glory to God through the church. Above all, continue to serve our Lord and Savior Jesus Christ through faith, hope and love.[11]

Walter Monroe wrote:

When one has a chance to draw nearer to another person through a shared experience, it gives the person a rare and choice opportunity to touch another person's feelings, humanity, and the sheerest joy of getting through the sunny side of the journey, or the soberest knowledge of being born by the Greatest power of God when the path has met with pain or loss or darkness.[12]

---

[10]*The Vine*, December 1997.
[11]Women's Day Program. (Frazier) May 18, 2003.
[12]Monroe, The Good News Journal, (Monroe), Jan 2007.

Although Jerome F. DelPino left the pulpit in the early forties, he revisited the church with these written words at the centennial observance of Stewart Memorial:

> Jesus never did concern himself with national nor
> racial background. They were people with prob-
> lems and people who needed spiritual guidance.
> If we are really seeking to guide others in the art
> of living together, we need information and sound
> thinking. We need religious techniques, the Bible,
> experience and the guidance of the Holy Spirit.[13]

Good Methodists, at times, need to be reminded of their
pledge to uphold the church with their prayers, presence, gifts
and service. William Higgins reminded us that as Christians,
we are called upon to be good stewards.

> Nothing is ours to keep for ourselves! Money, tal-
> ent, time, whatever we possess, is only ours to use.
> This is the great law written everywhere. No one
> owns anything for himself or herself alone, and no
> one can live to himself alone or herself alone! May
> God's blessing continue to grace Stewart Memorial
> United Methodist Church.[14]

---

[13] Stewart Memorial United Methodist Church,100th Anniversary Celebration, March 14, 1993.

[14] Church Bulletin, Oct. 4, 1970.

Chapter 25

Meeting the Challenge

Stewart Memorial began near the end of the nineteenth century, and as Daytona Beach and the United States grew and experienced changes, so did the church. Its founding in 1893 occurred 17 years after the incorporation of Daytona (later became Daytona Beach). Problems that could be identified with early Daytona also were those of early Stewart Memorial. Recalling the poor lighting, inadequate water, uncomfortable seating, and near-primitive means of transportation, one has every reason to rejoice over the current facilities available for worship. Almost in no way can the old Stewart Chapel be compared with the Stewart Memorial of today. If earlier church members could return, they would be confused about the name changes of their beloved church, and they would want to be told, again and again, how the church survived economic challenges, several wars, hurricanes, and "racial" or sexual discrimination. In 2006, Stewart Memorial remains strong in spite of its many obstacles.

Change of Names

The name given the church shortly after its founding in 1893 was *Stewart Chapel Methodist Episcopal Church*. It was named in honor of William Stewart, a generous donor, whose gift made possible the first sanctuary owned by the church. After his death, the name of the church was changed to *Stewart Memorial Methodist Episcopal Church*. That name was maintained until 1939 when the word Episcopal was dropped from its title following the unification of the three branches of Methodism. At that time, the local church became *Stewart Memorial Methodist Church*. The most recent change of names occurred in 1968, following the merger of the Methodist Church with the Evangelical United Brethren Church. At that time the name of the church was changed to *Stewart Memorial United Methodist Church*.

Economic Changes

Like other institutions, Stewart Memorial reacted to economic conditions in the state and nation. The economic depression of the 1930s affected the well-being of the church. The collection plate represented the difficulties the members of the congregation were encountering. Like many of the other churches of that day, the pastor, probably had to settle for food items, in some cases, rather than a generous salary. Stewart Memorial struggled through these hard times, and with cut backs in terms of services, extra rallies and church loans, the church survived.

Hurricanes

Hurricanes are rather commonplace in Florida. A 120-mile per hour hurricane struck just off the coast of Daytona Beach in August of the year of the founding of Stewart Memorial, and an eighty-miles per hour storm hit the city in September of 1894. The next hurricanes did not appear until 1921, when on October 25, a 90 mph hurricane visited the city.[1] For Stewart Memorial, the 75 miles per hour hurricane of July 28, 1926 was devastating. It tore down the unfinished walls of the new sanctuary that

---

[1]Daytona   Beach   Florida   Hurricanes, <http://www.hurricanecity.com/city/daytona.htm>.

was being constructed.[2] Hurricanes also appeared October. 19, 1950 and on Sept 11, 1960. Three hurricanes affected Daytona Beach during the summer of 2004 causing minor damage, but interfered with services at the church. Through the years, Stewart Memorial has reacted to the effects of hurricanes, having to pay for damages that occurred, and contributing to aid churches and people who were most affected.

Following the devastation in South Dade County caused by Hurricane Andrew, the Stewart Memorial congregation contributed $443.27 to assist storm victims. Members of the church made additional contributions through the Florida Conference and the American Red Cross.[3]

Stewart Memorial rallied to the aid of hurricane victims in Haiti following a major storm there. Mary Fears led the drive to send supplies to people in the wake of the tropical disaster.[4]

In addition to collections taken by UMCOR (United Methodist Committee on Relief) to help the victims of Hurricane Katrina, Stewart Memorial members sought to help persons who came to this area following the devastation. Typical of help was the preparing of a basket for a family which relocated here because of the hurricane. Canned goods, fruits, fresh vegetables, a turkey or ham were among the items solicited, as well as financial contributions. Sallie Culver led the effort.[5]

War and Wartime Regulations

Stewart Memorial, like the rest of the nation, suffered from the several wars in which the United States was involved: World War I, World War II, Korean War, War in Vietnam, Wars in Iraq, and other military conflicts. Members of the church were called upon to defend the country. Through the years, many mem-

---

[2]Historical account.
[3]*SMUMC News*, September 1992.
[4]Communications from Mrs. Mary Fears.
[5]Church Bulletin, December 11, 2005.

bers participated in the armed forces. At least one sacrificed his life for this patriotic cause. Lance Corporal Nathaniel Jenkins, a U. S. Marine was killed on October 23, 1983 from injuries received while serving in Beruit, Lebanon. He was awarded posthumously the Marine Corps Expeditionary Medal and Purple Heart. Not only was the church affected by those who were called to serve, but also by regulations which limited travel because of gas rationing. Services of the church also were curtailed because of limits placed on the use of lights.

Breaking Sexual Barriers

During the first few decades of its existence, Stewart Memorial existed in an environment where women were fighting for equal rights. In 1920, the women activists won a major victory when with the passage and ratification of the 19th Amendment to the U.S. Constitution, women obtained the same right to vote as men. This victory might have been only ceremonial, since African-American men were often denied the right to vote. Nevertheless, the adoption of the 19th Amendment necessitated changes in the church.

When Stewart Memorial was founded in 1893, women had few constitutional rights, and that was reflected in the positions women held in the church. Through the years, sexual discrimination has been modified. By 1926, Mary McLeod Bethune had joined a group of men as a trustee of Stewart Memorial. Perhaps, the greatest sexual barrier at the church was broken in 1995 when Joreatha Capers became the first female pastor. Shortly afterward, Sheila Flemming became the first female to be elected as charge lay leader for the church. Sallie Shelton Culver broke sexual barriers when she became the first female to serve as chair of the Administrative Board (1995-1998), and Wealthy Crooms was the first female to head the Trustee Board.

In order to monitor the progress in eliminating sexual discrimination in the United Methodist Church, the Status and Role of Women was established as a specialized ministry. In 2006, it was chaired by Paulette Monroe. Sexual discrimination against African-American women is a subject considered by the Black Methodists for Church Renewal (BMCR), although the problem of "racial" discrimination is the group's major concern. In his questions to the National BMCR in 1993, Rev. and Mrs. Carrill Munnings inquired: What is the role of the African-American female in our churches and How do we empower them and respond to the changing reality of African-American women?[6]

Overcoming "Racial" Obstacles

When informed persons consider the errors the Methodist Church has made regarding "racial" issues, they can better understand the reservation some African-American members feel towards "race" relations in the church. In recent years, the United Methodist Church has sought to confront some of these problems. In regard to appointments, one can point to the selection of William Ferguson as superintendent of the Deland District of the Florida Conference in 1980 as a major breakthrough. A tragic death, however, prevented him from completing his term.[7] In 1983, Ernest Newman, who later was elevated to bishop, became the second African American to hold the top position in the Deland District.[8] Stewart Memorial viewed it as a major victory in 1996, when Cornelius Henderson of Covington, GA, a long time visitor to Daytona Beach, was named Resident Bishop of the Florida Conference.

While it was good news when African Americans were appointed to high positions in the Florida Conference and the Deland District, the news was even better when those assigned were members of Stewart Memorial. In 1972, Richard V. Moore was honored by the Florida Conference (UMC) when he was

---

[6]Rev. & Mrs. C. S. Munnings, Sr., 1993 National BMCR Questions and Issues, March 15-20, 1993.

[7]*Florida Flame*, 368-369, 398.

[8]Ibid., 369, 398.

named charge lay leader.[9] Before this assignment, he was the Conference lay leader under the old Central Jurisdiction. Harry Burney, Jr. was later selected lay leader of the Deland District. Joel Fears, Sr. broke "racial" barriers when he was selected president of the Deland District of the United Methodist Men in 1987.[10] Also of significance was the appointment of Sallie Shelton Culver to the chairmanship of the Board of Trustees of the United Methodist Children's Home in 2001.[11] Henrine Ward Banks broke "racial" barriers when she was elected president of the Deland District United Methodist Women in 1975.[12]

African Americans are continuing their efforts to bring about "racial" justice in the United Methodist Church through the National Black Methodists for Church Renewal (BMCR). Four of the purposes of this Black Caucus are:

- To empower and involve Black Methodists for effective witness and service among pastors, laity in local churches, conferences and schools, and the larger community.

- To encourage and involve Black Methodists and others in the struggle for economic and social justice.

- To expose latent and overt forms of racism in all local, regional, and national agencies and institutions of The United Methodist Church.

- To act as an agitating conscience on all boards and agencies of The United Methodist Church in order to keep them sensitive to the needs and expressions of a "genuinely" inclusive and relevant church.[13]

---

[9] *Florida Flame*, 359.

[10] Information from Joel Fears.

[11] Memorandum from Mrs. Sallie Shelton-Culver.

[12] "Henrine Ward Banks Dead at 73," *Daytona Evening News*, April 24, 1980.

[13] Racial Ethnic Concern. <http://www.gcorr.org/commiittee_files/BlackConstituency/

Most of the recent pastors of Stewart Memorial have played active roles in the BMCR. Responding to the 1993 National BMCR Questions and Issues, Rev. & Mrs. Munnings posed these questions: "How do we establish a vision (from the conference level) for our African-American church?" and "What are the best models for church growth in the United Methodist African-American Church?"[14]

Pastors of Stewart Memorial have participated in the BMCR chapter of the Florida Conference since its beginning in 1994. In undated documents listing top bullet points to strengthen the African-American Church, Kevin James Sr. listed: advocates for justice and equality and opportunities for African-American male clergy in the Florida Annual Conference and the church at large.[15] Michael Frazier listed: church education about new and exciting ministries that could change the direction of traditional churches.[16] Walter Monroe was concerned about the recruitment and training of young men and women for the ministry. He viewed the early identification of these potential leaders and giving them the necessary guidance as essential to the process of preparing new leaders.[17]

Pastors of Stewart Memorial have held key positions that enabled them to wage struggles for "racial" justice. In 1991, when Alfonso Delaney chaired the Florida Conference Commission on Religion and Race, he gave awards to four churches for their Inclusiveness Ministry.[18] Carrill Munnings chaired the Commission on Religion and Race, and from 1992–1995, he led the Florida Conference Commission on Religion and Race.[19] During Joreatha Capers's tenure at Stewart Memorial, she was involved with the re-organization of the Florida Caucus of Black Methodists for Church Renewal (BMCR) and served as the Vice

---

[14]Munnings.

[15]Questionnaire of Dr, Kevin James (Church's Office).

[16]Questionnaire of Rev. Frazier (Church's Office).

[17]Conversation with Dr. Walter Monroe.

[18]*SMUMC News*, July 1991.

[19]Memo from Rev. Carrill Munnings.

Chairperson. During her stay in Nashville, she contributed to the cause of Blacks when she worked as Assistant General Secretary Black College Fund and Ethnic Concerns at the General Board of Higher Education and Ministry (1996-2005). Currently, she is serving on the African-American Plan Task Force for Florida Conference.[20]

A church can be credited with serving its purpose when it successfully weathers the many storms it faces. Such has been the life of Stewart Memorial. Economic depressions, wars, hurricanes, racism, and sexism were forces which sought to derail it, but none was successful. It came out of its first century as a powerful instrument, and with its historic record and faith in the future, this second century, although a challenge, promises to be one of achievement. For these blessings, Stewart Memorial is grateful to God, Almighty, and it looks forward to continue to build on the wings of faith.

Walking to church was an inconvenience,
But it could not stop us from worshiping the Lord.
For greater was the time we had for fellowship,
And acting together in one accord.

Inadequate was the lighting of our church
And uncomfortable were the pews of wood.
Many other discouragements we constantly faced,
In striving for a cause we knew to be good.

Affected we were by economic conditions—
With debts we owed very difficult to pay.
When with wars and hurricanes we were confronted,
To God, always, we turned to pray.

Against injustices, we waged many struggles,
All types of discriminations we tried to defeat,
Our youth always, we tried to encourage,
From our Christian commitment, we'll never retreat.

---

[20]Memo from Dr. Joreatha Capers, June 30, 2007.

Challenges of the past we successfully encountered,
But more in the future we are sure to face.
Overcome them we will if we trust in God,
Who extends to us his mercy and grace.

Appendix A – Bishops

Bishops Who Presided over Stewart Memorial since 1921

South Florida Mission Conference

E. G. Richardson 1921-22
Ernest L. Waldorf 1923
E. G. Richardson 1924-25
Luther B. Wilson 1926
Joseph F. Berry 1927
E. G. Richardson 1928
Fred T. Keeney 1929
William E. Brown 1930
Charles L. Mead 1931
Fred T. Keeney 1932-34
Robert Jones 1935
Fred T. Keeney 1936
Charles W. Flint 1937
G. Bromley Oxnam 1938
Edgar Blake 1939

South Florida Conference (Central Jurisdiction) Methodist Church

A. P. Shaw 1940
L. H. King 1941-1945
R. N. Brooks 1946

E.W. Kelly 1947-48
J. W. E. Bowen 1949-1952

Florida Conference (Central Jurisdiction) Methodist Church

J. W. E. Bowen 1953-1960
M. L. Harris 1961- 1966
James W. Henley 1966-67
Edgar A. Scott 1967-68
Allen A. Scott 1968-69
James W. Henley 1969-1970

Florida Conference (Southeastern Jurisdiction) United Methodist Church

James W. Henley 1970-1973
Joel D. McDavid 1973-1981
Earl G. Hunt, Jr. 1981-1987
H. Hasbrouck Hughes, Jr. 1987-1996
Cornelius L. Henderson 1996-1999
James Lloyd Knox, 1999-2001
Timothy W. Whitaker 2001-

Appendix B – District Superintendents

District Superintendents Who Presided Over Stewart Memorial

South Florida Conference - East Coast

> 1917 S. A. Huger
> 1918 H. W. Bartley

South Florida Conference - Atlantic

> 1921 J. A. Simpson
> 1927 J.W. Wesley
> 1928 W. O. Bartley
> 1929 D. W. Demps
> 1934 H. W. Bartley
> 1936 D. S. Selmore
> 1937 S. D. Bankston
> 1943 O. A. Burns
> 1946 Aaron Hall

Florida Conference – Atlantic (Central Jurisdiction)

> 1953 Aaron Hall
> 1955 Frank Cambridge
> 1962 E. J. Shepherd

Florida Conference – South Florida (CJ)

> 1964 E. J. Shepherd
> 1968 Cubell A. Johnson

District Superintendents - Deland District

> J. Wilburn McLeod
> Walter B. Rutland
> J. Lloyd Knox
> William M. Ferguson
> Eugene West (Interim)
> Ernest Newman
> William L. Brackman, Jr.
> Donald F, Padgett
> Montfort C. Duncan, Jr.
> Jeffrey Stiggins
> Wayne Curry

District Superintendent East Central District

> Wayne Wiatt

Appendix C – Pastors

Pastors of Stewart Memorial in Approximate Order of Pastoral Charge

Thomas H. B. Walker, D.D.
J.S. Middleton
L.J. Littles
O.B. Jackson
Albert Emanuel
H.W. Austin
B.J. Shannon
O.M. Irving
Scott Bartley
G.B. Wilson
D.S. Selmore
Joseph M. Dees
G.B. Lennon
Matthew Walker Clair, Jr. (Bishop)
J. W. Moultrie
W. P. Pickens
J.S. Yedd
Thomas A. Huger
J.W. Killer
Harry L. Burney, Sr.
James L. Todd
S.D. Bankston
C.R.A. Banks

Jerome F. Delpino
A.C. Trice
H.D. McLain
Evans Hurley
Rogers P. Fair, Sr.
James C. Murray
John H. Adams, Jr.
Arthur Crowell
Eddie J. Rivers, Jr.
Sylvester Gillespie
Rogers P. Fair, Sr.
William Higgins,
Rogers P. Fair, Sr.
Eddie J. Rivers, Jr.
Alfonso Delaney
Carrill S. Munnings, Sr.
Joreatha Capers,
Kevin James, Sr.
Michael Frazier, Sr.
Eddie J. Rivers,
Walter Eugene Monroe, Jr.
Miriti Silas M'Mworia

The above list was taken from the historic sketches found in *The Celebration of the Forty-Fourth Anniversary of Stewart Memorial Methodist Episcopal Church, Souvenir Program*, December 15-19, 1937; and *Stewart Memorial United Methodist Church, 100th Anniversary Celebration*, March 14, 1993.

Available biographies and notes on church-related activities of former pastors' information of the early period are limited.

Thomas Hamilton Beb Walker – Thomas Hamilton Beb Walker, the son of Elizabeth and F. D. Walker, was born July 15, 1873 in Tallahassee, FL. After a four year stay, he graduated from Cookman Institute in Jacksonville, FL. Later, he graduated from Gammon Theological Seminary in Atlanta, GA. Hamilton received honorary doctorates from the College of West Africa, and the College of Liberia.

Figure 25.1:
Walker

Walker is noted for his ministerial work, having entered the Methodist ministry at the age of 16, and holding pastoral charges in many of the larger churches in his district. He is credited with founding the St Joseph Aid Society, an organization which had more than 150,000 members by 1927 in cities throughout the United States. He also edited the *Church and Society World*, a sixty four page magazine.

In addition to being a clergyman, Walker was a writer, having written such books as *The Man Without Blemish* (1902), *Egyptology* (1906), *Bobby the Victorian Preacher* (1906), *Aunt Dysie's Vision of Hell* (1910), *The Revelations of Epic* (1912), and *The Presidents of Liberia* (1915). He was also the editor of the *Seven Star Banner*, and the *Quarterly Review*.

Matthew Walker Clair, Jr. – Matthew Walker Clair, Jr., the son of Bishop Matthew Clair, Sr. and Fannie Walker Clair, was born August 12, 1890 at Harper's Ferry, West Virginia. He attended Syracuse University, received his AB degree from Howard University in 1915, and his S.T.B. from Boston University in 1918. Gammon Seminary conferred upon him the Doctor of Divinity degree in 1936.

Before accepting the pastoral charge of Stewart Memorial (1924-25), he served in Bedford, VA, Martinsburg, WV, and Roanoke, VA. He also served as a chaplain in the U. S. Army during the First World War. Following his tenure in Daytona Beach, FL, Clair served as pastor in Denver, CO, and Indianapolis, IN before accepting several positions with the Board of Missions of the Methodist Episcopal Church, and a position at Gammon Theological Seminary as professor of Practical Theology.

Finally, he served a pastoral charge at St. Mark Methodist Episcopal Church in Chicago, IL.

The Central Jurisdiction elected Clair bishop in 1952. He was sent by the Council of Bishops to "review and appraise Methodist work" in Africa from January to April, 1954, in Central and South America from September to December 1958, and in Europe in 1961. He also was a delegate to the Southeast Asia Central Conference in Singapore in 1956.

Clair, Jr. was president of the College of Bishops of the Central Jurisdiction (1960-62), and was chairman of the Commission to Study Faith and War in the Nuclear Age. He was also a member of the General Board of Education of the Board of Christian Social Concerns of the Commission on Promotion and Cultivation, the Commission on Church Union, the Commission on Ecumenical Consultation, and a member of the General Board and General Assembly of the National Council of Churches. Clair, Jr. retired in 1964 and died July 10, 1968.

(Who's Who in the Methodist Church, 1966, reprinted in Encyclopedia of World Methodism, 511-512)

Thomas Albert Huger – Thomas Albert Huger, son of a pioneer Methodist minister, was born in Key West, Florida. He graduated from Gammon Theological Seminary and was granted an honorary doctorate from Edward Waters College. After entering the Florida Conference in 1921, he served on many Boards, Commissions and Committees. Huger held pastorates in Gainesville, Jacksonville, Ocala, West Palm Beach, and Daytona Beach. He served as superintendent of the Gulf District in 1942 and later of the Jacksonville District. Huger died in Lakeland, Florida on January 13, 1970 at the age of 76. He was the father of James Huger of Stewart Memorial.

Figure 25.2: Huger

Clarence Russell Andrew Banks – Clarence Russell An-

drew Banks (better known as C. R. A. Banks), the son of Anna
Mae Willis and Fred Douglas Banks was born in Hannibal, Missouri, March 3, 1895. After receiving his high school education
in Chicago, he attended Clark College and Gammon Theological Seminary in Atlanta, GA.

At the age of sixteen, while a member of the Centennial
United Methodist Church, Banks was licensed to preach. His
first pastoral assignment was at Farrington, Missouri in 1927.
The following year he moved to a church in Cedar Key, FL.
During his thirty-nine year tenure in Florida, he held pastoral
charges at some of the leading United Methodist churches, including St Johns UMC in Fort Lauderdale where he served for
sixteen years. He also served two terms as District Superintendent of the South Florida District of the Florida Conference.
(C.J.) Banks retired from active ministry in 1967, but served as
supply minister for two additional years. He died on October
23, 1971.

Jerome F. Del Pino – Jerome F. Del Pino, a native of
Tampa, Florida, was born in 1913. His education was received
at Clafin College Pastoral Training Center, Alabama State
College, and Garrett Theological Seminary in Evanston, IL. He
undertook further study at Northwestern, Yale and American
Universities. His early employment included minister at
Bethel United Methodist Church in Plant City and director
of Religious Education at Bethune-Cookman College. Later
he pastored the following churches: Palen United Methodist
Church (UMC) in Savannah, GA, Asbury and Wesley UMC
in Lexington, KY, Camphor Memorial UMC in St Paul MN,
and Wiley Memorial UMC in Chattanooga, TN. Del Pino also
served as chaplain at Morristown College and the Memorial
Hospital in Morristown,TN and after retirement, as chaplain
of St. Paul Ramsey Hospital. He also served as secretary of
both the South Florida Conference and the Savannah Georgia
Conference of the UMC.

Evan M. Hurley – Evan Hurley, a long-time Methodist
minister, transferred to the Florida Conference from the Savan-

nah Conference in 1920. Since that time he has held several pastoral charges, including those at Stewart Memorial of Daytona Beach and Ebenezer United Methodist of Jacksonville, Florida. At the time of his death in 1920 he was the Superintendent of the Jacksonville District.

Rogers P. Fair, Sr. – Dr. Rogers P. Fair, the son of Eugene Robert and Julia Fair, was born in Greenwood, SC. He received his Bachelor's degree at Clark College in Atlanta and his Master of Arts degree from Atlanta University. He began his ministerial work in the South Carolina Conference, and transferred to the Florida Conference in 1946 to accept the appointment as pastor of Stewart Memorial. Except for a brief ministerial assignment at the Trinity United Methodist Church in West Palm Beach, Fair's pastoral charge has been limited to Stewart Memorial. He also served as chaplain of Bethune-Cookman College for many years.

Figure 25.3: Fair

Fair was active in the Methodist Church when African-American churches were restricted to its Central Jurisdiction. He served as secretary to the Florida Conference (CJ) for four years. Later, as a part of the Florida Conference of the United Methodist Church, he served as a member of the Committee on Higher Education and Campus Ministry, and the Committee on Memoirs. Fair also served on the Board of Ministry of the Deland District.

Fair established international credentials, participating in the Institute of Methodist Theological Studies at Oxford University, England in 1958, 1965, and 1973; Studies in World Peace which convened at Moscow University in the Soviet Union, 1965, 1975 and 1982; and Studies in Promoting Enduring Peace in Germany, Poland, France, Czechoslovakia, and Switzerland 1983. Fair was chosen by the American Delegation as preacher in the Soviet Union, Poland, and South

Korea. He also was a delegate to the 1986 World Methodist Conference, which convened in Nairobi, Kenya.

Outside the realm of the United Methodist Church, Fair has participated in a variety of religious activities. He was the first African American to head the Halifax Ministerial Association. Among his many honors: an honorary doctorate from Bethune-Cookman College and a listing in *Who's Who among American Clergymen* (1973-1985).

John Hubert Adams, Jr. – John Hubert Adams, Jr., the son of Laura Ward and John Hubert Adams, Sr. was born in Martin, Florida, January 13, 1919. He attended Fessenden Academy in Martin, Howard Academy in Ocala and graduated from Campbell Street High in Daytona Beach. His higher education was at Bethune-Cookman College, Morehouse College and Gammon Theological Seminary.

After entering the Florida Conference (CJ) as an elder, he served pastoral charges in Arcadia and Bradenton before being assigned to Stewart Memorial. Following his tenure here, he served in Ocala, Clearwater and St. Petersburg. After these assignments, he held pastoral charges in Illinois from 1970 – 1979. Upon his return to the Florida Conference, he served in Melbourne, Gainesville, Tyler Temple in Tampa, and churches in Reddick, and High Springs. Adams retired in 1989 and died January 3, 1997.

Arthur R. Crowell – Arthur R. Crowell was born in Columbus, Georgia, June 29, 1918. He graduated from Wilberforce University with a B. S. degree, and he received the Bachelor of Divinity degree from Payne Theological Seminary of Wilberforce. His Master of Arts degree and professional diploma in administration were earned at Columbia University of New York. He has done additional work at Union Theological Seminary of New York, and Garrett Theological Seminary of Evanston, Illinois. He was awarded an honorary doctorate degree by Jackson Theological Seminary.

Crowell was ordained a deacon in 1940, and an elder in 1942 at Wilberforce. He transferred to the South Carolina Conference in 1948, and worked there until he joined the Florida Annual Conference in 1957. While in the latter, he held pastoral charges at Scott Church in Melbourne, Trinity in Daytona Beach, and Trinity in St. Augustine prior to his pastorate at Stewart Memorial (1964 -66). He then was appointed District Superintendent of the Central Florida District (1966 to 1969). From 1969 to 1972, Crowell served as associate program director of the Florida Conference. He concluded his affiliation with the Florida Conference with a pastoral charge at Trinity UMC in West Palm Beach (1972 –1974). In 1974 he transferred to the New York Conference.

Figure 25.4:
Rivers

Eddie J. Rivers, Jr. – Eddie J. Rivers, Jr. was born in St Petersburg, Florida, but grew up in Alachua County. He received his Bachelor's Degree at Clark (now Clark-Atlanta) University, and his Master of Divinity Degree from Gammon Theological Seminary.

Before his first tenure at Stewart Memorial in 1955-1961, he served as assistant pastor of Warren UMC in Atlanta and Pleasant Hill UMC in Arcadia Florida. After his first tenure at Stewart Memorial, he served as pastor of Ebenezer UMC in Jacksonville and then as superintendent of the Sarah Hunt Children's Home in Daytona Beach. Following his stay at the Children's Home, Rivers served as associate pastor of St. Paul UMC in Tampa, prior to assuming the pastorate of Tyler Temple UMC (Tampa), Ocala Parish UMC, and St John UMC in Fort Lauderdale. He returned to Daytona Beach to assume for the second time the pastoral charge of Stewart Memorial (1986-1990). Following this tenure he retired after forty years, but returned to active service as retired supply pastor of Trinity UMC in Sanford, FL. He served his third pastoral charge at Stewart Memorial from 2004-2005. He died a week after his final retirement.

Rivers was the recipient of an honorary doctorate from Edward Waters College, and is listed in *Who is Who* of the United Methodist Church.

He served on the FC Committee on Worship, History and Archives, and Diaconal Ministry.

William Higgins – William Higgins received his bachelor's degree from Bethune-Cookman College, and his DDS from Meharry Medical School. He entered the ministry while engaged in a successful dental practice in Palatka, Florida.

Higgins served as Pastor of Palen Methodist in Savannah, Ga. Afterward he attended Gammon Theological Seminary (ITC), while holding pastoral charges at St. Stephens Memorial Church in Hastings and St. John's in Crescent City, Florida. Other churches which he pastored included: St. Paul's in Tampa, Stewart Memorial in Daytona Beach, Trinity in Lake City and Emanuel in Palatka. Higgins also served as the United Methodist Church's chaplain at Lake Butler Correctional Center.

Rev Alfonso Delaney – Alfonso Delaney began his college education at Morristown College in Morristown, TN, where he received his Associate Arts degree prior to entering Bethune-Cookman College and completed his undergraduate education. After receiving his Bachelor's Degree, he attended and received a Master of Divinity from the Interdenominational Theological Seminary in Atlanta, GA. Delaney received his Ph. D. degree from Cornerstone University in Dallas, Texas,

Before his pastoral charge at Stewart Memorial, Delaney held a pastoral charge at Zion UMC in Clearwater. He left Stewart to become pastor of Ebenezer UMC in Miami, FL. While in the Florida Conference, he chaired the Conference Commission on Religion and Race.

Carrill S. Munnings – Carrill S. Munnings, the son of
Charles and Elizabeth S. Munnings, received his Bachelor of
Science Degree from the University of Kansas, and his Master
of Divinity from Gammon Theological Seminary. Prior to his
pastoral charge at Stewart Memorial, he served at Mt. Zion
UMC in Clearwater FL.

Figure 25.5:
Munnings

During his tenure at Stewart Memorial, he served as Chairperson of the
Commission on Religion and Race, and
led the Florida Conference Commission
on Religion and Race from 1992 to 1995,
shortly after he left Stewart Memorial.
While in Daytona Beach, Munnings
taught religion and Bible classes at
Bethune-Cookman College, and he led
and taught a pre-seminarian discipleship
group. Munnings was also involved in
ecumenical affairs—leading community
pastors in a combined 3-hour Good
Friday noon worship service of drama and preaching from the
seven last words of Jesus.

Following his tenure at Stewart Memorial, he served as pastor of Trinity UMC in West Palm Beach.

Joreatha M. Capers – Joreatha Capers broke the sexual
barrier in becoming the first female pastor of Stewart Memorial. She left the position here to accept the position of Assistant
General Secretary for the Black College Fund and Ethnic Concerns at the General Board of Higher Education and Ministry,
Nashville, TN (1996-2005). In 2005, she returned to Florida
and accepted the pastoral charge of Ebenezer United Methodist
Church, Miami, Florida, where she is currently serving. Prior
to leaving for Nashville, TN, she served on the Council of Finance and Administration (C F & A) of the Florida Conference,
and upon her return to Florida, she was re-elected to C F & A
in 2000, and is currently serving. According to Capers, **Hope**,
Empowerment and **Reconciliation** characterize her ministry.

Kevin James – Kevin James was born in Los Angeles, CA, but was reared in Daytona Beach, Florida. He received his Bachelor's Degree from Bethune-Cookman College, with a major in religion and philosophy and his Master of Divinity from the Interdenominational Theological Seminary.

He served as an assistant minister at Stewart Memorial under Rogers P. Fair. Later, he was appointed pastor of Emmanuel United Methodist Church in Palatka, Florida, and as campus minister at Florida A. & M. University. Upon the retirement of Fair, he was named chaplain of Bethune-Cookman College. Shortly thereafter, he was assigned pastor of Stewart Memorial. His dual assignment came to an end when he was appointed superintendent of the St. Petersburg District.

Figure 25.6: James

James has worked on the General Commission on United Methodist Men and as a part of the Florida Conference he has been a member of the Board of Ordained Ministry, Committee on Institute of Preaching, Administrative Review Committee, and Worship Committee.

Following his tenure as District Superintendent, James was named pastor of Palma Ceia UMC in Tampa, FL. He is a member of the Board of Trustees of Bethune-Cookman University and the Interdenominational Theological Seminary.

James was awarded an honorary doctorate from Bethune-Cookman College.

Michael Frazier, Sr. – Michael Frazier, Sr., a graduate of Bethune-Cookman College, received his Master of Divinity Degree from the Interdenominational Theological Seminary. Prior to his tenure as pastor of Stewart Memorial, he held the pastoral charge of Zion United Methodist in Ocala, Florida. In the Florida Conference, he has served on the Committee on Ministry and the Committee on Institute of Preaching.

Figure 25.7:
Frazier

Walter E. Monroe, Jr. – Walter E. Monroe, Jr., a native of Newport News, Virginia, was reared in Palatka, Florida. He is the recipient of two bachelor of art degrees, one from Bethune-Cookman College with an emphasis in religion and philosophy, and one from Bethany Bible College (Dothan, Alabama) with and emphasis on Biblical studies. He pursued graduate studies at the Candler School of Theology of Emory University (Atlanta, Georgia) where he received the Master of Divinity Degree with emphasis on pastoral care and Biblical studies. At that institution he also received certification in the Program of Black Church Studies.

Figure 25.8:
Monroe

Monroe began his ministry in the New York/Washington Conference of the United Methodist Church, but transferred to the Florida Annual Conference in 1982. Among the churches in which he held pastoral charge are Scott Chapel UMC in Melbourne, Lake City Parish UMC, Ebenezer and Grace UMC in Orlando, and University UMC in Gainesville. He also served as Director of Wesley Foundation of the University of Florida.

In the Florida Conference, Rev. Monroe serves on the Board of Trustees of the Florida United Methodist Children's Home,

Board of the United Methodist Foundation, Inc. and Board of Ordained Ministry.

He authored *Go Ahead and Visit* (A handbook on visitation) and *Changing Our Perspective About Death: An Introduction.*

Monroe was awarded honorary doctorates by Jameson Christian College and the United Theological Seminary.

Appendix D – Charge Lay Leaders

The lay leader is the "primary lay representative of the laity" in the local church. Among his responsibilities are to:

* foster awareness of the role of laity both within the congregation and through their ministries in the home, workplace, community and world and to find ways within the community of faith to recognize all these ministries

* meet regularly with the pastor to discuss the state of the church and the need for ministry. Among the lay leaders of Stewart Memorial were:

Figure 25.9:
Adams

Dr. Texas A. Adams – a local physician and founding physician of McLeod Hospital, who was one of the earlier members of Stewart Memorial. He held such prior positions as president of the Methodist Men, chairman of the Trustee Board and church treasurer.

Dr. Richard V. Moore – president of Bethune-Cookman College, served as lay leader. He also served as conference lay leader, both under the segregated Central Jurisdiction and for the integrated Florida Conference (UMC). Several times he was elected a delegate to both the Jurisdictional Conference and the General Conference. In 1966, he was a delegate to the World Conference on Methodism in London. He also served on the historic Commission of 1970 that eliminated mandated segregation in the United Methodist Church. He is listed in *Who's Who in Methodism.* He was a trustee of the Sarah Hunt Home. At Stewart Memorial, he served as a Trustee, lay speaker and as chair of the Building Fund.

Figure 25.10: Moore

Figure 25.11: Fears

Mr. Joel V. Fears, Sr. – replaced Dr. R.V. Moore as charge lay leader in 1994, and served until 2004. Again in 2006 he was asked to assume the position. He also serves as a lay speaker and scouting coordinator. Previously, he served as chairman of the Trustee Board, and Administrative Board. Fears also has served as District President of the United Methodist Men and District Lay leader, He serves/has served on several District and Conference committees, including: Committee on Superintendency, Committee on Ministry, Leadership Committee and District Committee on Lay Speaking. In the Florida Conference, Fears served on the Conference Board of Lay Members.

Dr. Sheila Flemming – former Dean of the School of Social Sciences at Bethune-Cookman College, served as lay leader from 2004 to 2006. She served the church in many roles. Prior to coming to Stewart Memorial she was employed as the associate general secretary in the Mission Personnel Resources Program of the United Methodist Church(1988-1990). In this capacity, she was responsible for the selection process of missionaries for the UMC. She also supervised the Crusade Scholarship Program for Graduate Training. She was very active in the Florida Conference, serving as chairperson for the work area on Church and Society. She also headed the Conference Bishop's Initiative on Children and Poverty in the Deland District.

Appendix E – In Memory

In Memory of Our Deceased Members (Dec. 2006)

Stewart Memorial began near the end of the Nineteenth Century, and as Daytona Beach, Florida, and the United States grew and experienced changes, so did the church.

Adams, Lodosca
Adams, Rosa
Adams, Susie W.
Adams, Texas A., MD
Alexander, Bertha
Alexander, Lena Warren
Alexander, Olaf G.
Allum, Ella
Anderson, Anna
Anglin, Elnora
Anglin, J.H..
Anglin, William A.
Bain, Annie
Baker, Bertha Slack
Banks, Henrine W.
Banks, Rowena
Barnett, Hattie
Barron, Astride Dyett
Bartley, H.E., MD
Bartley, Margaret
Bazzell, Leroy, Sr.
Bell, Lelia Williams
Bell, Richard

Bergman, Otis
Bergman, Winnie
Bethune, Dr. Mary McLeod
Bolen, Marie
Brigety, Jr. Rev. Carl E.
Briggs, Clyde & Pearl
Brooks, Rosa Burrows
Brooks, Rufus
Brown, Earl N., DDS
Brown, Earlyn
Brown, Kenneth
Brown, Wynona Mason
Burgess, Roberta
Burgess, David
Burney, Iona
Burney, Jr. Harry L.
Burns, Arthur L., Jr.
Burns, Sarah B.
Burrows, Dr. Felix
Byrd, Idella
Caruthers, Bobbie
Chambers, Verla
Chambers, Willie

Jenkins, Cornelius W.
Jenkins, LCpl. Nathaniel
Jones, Alphonso.
Jones, Benjamin
Jones, Homer
Jones, Lucille D.C.
Jones, Myrtle Olivia
Jones, Olivia Anderson
Jones, Victor
Jones, Williams
Kirksey, Constance
Kirsey, Samuel
Latimore, Agnes
Latimore, O.J.
Lee, Bertram
Leggett, Agnes
Leonard, Eilean
Lewis, Leroy
Lewis, Lillie
Lewis, Lucien
Liferidge, Moses
Lucas, Rosa
Mann, Josh
Mann, Lugenia
Martin, Herman
Mathis, Charles
McClain, H.C.
McClendon, Hazelean
McClendon. Willie
McDaniel, Reginald
McDaniel, Robert
McDaniel, Ruth W.
McGee, Margaret
Micken, Alice
Miller, Jerona
Mitchell, Jessie M.
Nicholson, Jennie
O'Rouke, Wilnette
Oliver, Pinkie
Parsons, William

Perkins, Dorothy S.
Perkins, Sadie
Pete, Maude
Peterson, Mildred
Pettway, Eunice
Pettway, Nelse
Pyles, Bertha
Rivers, Dr. Eddie J., Jr.
Rivers, Ida
Rivers, Nathaniel
Rivers, Ophelia
Roane, Dr. Florence
Roberson, Luvert
Roberts, Lottie M.
Rodriquez, Edward
Romeo, Maggie R.
Rowe, Beatrice.
Ruff, Daisy B.
Ruff, Dewey
Sanders, Minnie
Shears, C.B.
Slacks, J. Leroy
Slacks, Louise Kelly
Slacks, William
Slaughter, Gwendolyn
Smith, Jil
Smith, Ella
Smith, Beulah
Smith, Beverly
Smith, Joseph
Smith, Lillian
Smith, Palmsy
Smith, Shelly
Stanback, Dr. Therman
Stewart, Phillip, M.D.
Temple, Maxine
Thomas, Katherine
Thompson, Herbert W., Sr.
Thompson, Olga
Tiller, Joelita.

Toombs, Gladys M.
Trapp, Cleo
Trapp, E. P.
Trapp, Lucille
Tynes, Calvin
Tynes, Olive
Tyson, Marcus
Van Pool, Edward
Van Pool, Marie
Ward, Lester

Warren, Charles
Webb, Clara
Wells, Joe N.
Whitehead, Georgia
Williams, Derrick R.
Williams, Eloise E.
Williams, Ines
Willis, Hattie E. D.
Wilson, Theodore

Appendix F – Dates in History

Dates in the History of Stewart Memorial United Methodist Church

1893: Founding of Stewart Memorial Methodist Episcopal Church by Rev. Thomas H. B. Walker (Stewart Chapel was original name)

1935: Cornerstone Laying for the Old Stewart Memorial (now Richard V. Moore Center)

December 15 -19, 1937: Forty-Fourth Anniversary of Stewart Memorial

1939: Stewart Memorial Methodist Episcopal Church was renamed Stewart Memorial Methodist Church

August 7-13, 1950: Fifty-Seventh Anniversary of Stewart Memorial Methodist Church 1893 -1950 and the Fourth Anniversary of the Pastor Rev. Rogers Pressley Fair, Sr. 1946-1950

October 3, 1957: Death of Dr. Texas A. Adams

1969 Stewart Memorial Methodist Church was re-named Stewart Memorial United Methodist Church

May, 21, 1972: Groundbreaking Ceremonies For the Proposed Stewart Memorial United Methodist

Church

April 15, 1973: Celebration: A Service of Consecration and Open House, Stewart Memorial United
Methodist Church

April 5, 1981: The Burning of the Mortgage in a
Service of Thanksgiving and Holy Communion

March 14, 1993: 100th Anniversary Celebration of
Stewart Memorial

January 8, 1994: Funeral of Dr. Richard V. Moore,
Sr.

April 5, 2004: Funeral of Reverend Dr. Rogers P.
Fair

July 15, 2005: Funeral of Reverend Dr. Eddie
James Rivers.

Special Sundays and Program Events of 1998

January
Call to Prayer and Self-Denial (Jan-March Choose a Date
within these Months) United Methodist Women
Epiphany: Evangelism and Worship
Human Relations Day: Religion and Race, Church and So-
ciety, Missions, Admin. Council
M. L. King's Birthday: Special Events, Admin Council ,
Religion and Race
Week of Prayer & Christian Unity: Committee on Christian
Unity
Ecumenical Sunday: Committee on Christian Unity
February
Black History Month: Religion and Race, Church & Soci-
ety, Mission, Worship
Boy Scout Sunday: Coordinator of Scouts & Youth
Ash Wednesday: Evangelism and Worship

Brotherhood/Sisterhood Week: Christian Unity and Interreligious Concerns

March

Women's History Month: Status of Women, Events Committee, Admin Council, Worship

World Day of Prayer: United Methodist Women

Girl Scout Sunday: Youth Coordinator, Scouting Coordinator

One Great Hour of Sharing (An offering should be sent), Missions

Passion/Palm Sunday: Worship

April

Religious in American Life Month: Worship

Holy Thursday/Maundy: Worship

Good Friday: Worship

Resurrection Sunday: Events Committee, Administratve Council, Worship

Consultation on Church Union: Interreligious Concerns & Christian Concerns

Native American Awareness Sunday (Offering), Campus Ministry, Administrative Council, Education Evangelism

Heritage Sunday: Events, Administrative Council, Education Evangelism

May

Christian Home Month: Administrative. Council, Events, Family Coordinator

National Day of Prayer: Administrative. Council, Events, Interreligious Concerns

May Fellowship Day: United Methodist Women

National Family Week: Family, Youth, & Children Coordinator, Admin Council, Events

Mother's Day: Administrative Council, Events

Pentecost: Evangelism, Worship, Christian Unity, Interreligious Concerns

Trinity Sunday Worship

Peace With Justice Sunday (Offering should be sent): Church & Society

June

Father's Day and Children's Day Family Coordinator, Events, Administrative Council

September

Grandparent's Day: Family Coordinator, Events, Administrative Council

October

World Communion Sunday (Offering): Council, Events, Mission, High Ed., Campus Ministry, Worship

Laity Sunday: Adult Coordinator, Lay Leader, Administrative Council, Events

Reformation Day: Christian Unity and Interreligious Concerns

November

All Saints Day: Worship

World Community Day: United Methodist Women

Bible Sunday: Evangelism and Education

National Bible Week: Evangelism

Thanksgiving: Worship and Mission

United Meth. Student Day (Offering should be sent): Higher Education & Campus Mininistry.

December

Christmas Eve/Christmas Day: Administrative Council Pastor, Events

Watch Night: Evangelism and Worship

Sources

AB: Administrative Board

AC: Administrative Council

BD: *The Book of Discipline of the United Methodist Church,* 1996

CB: Church Bulletin

Celebration: *Stewart Memorial United Methodist Church,100th Anniversary Celebration,* March 14, 1993.

Consecration Celebration: *A Service of Consecration and Open House, Stewart Memorial United Methodist Church,* April 15, 1973.

Directory: Program Calendar and Membership Directory

Groundbreaking: *Groundbreaking Ceremonies For the Proposed Stewart Memorial United Methodist Church* , May, 21, 1972.

Handbook: *Handbook of Stewart Memorial Methodist Church, 1893 -1947.*

Historical Data: H. C. McLain and Dr. T. A. Adams "Historical Data," *The Celebration of the Forty-Fourth Anniversary of Stewart Memorial Methodist Episcopal Church, December 15-19, 1937,* p. 3.

The Vine: *SMUMC, The Vine.*

Vision 2000: *Vision 2000 Document,* July 12, 1999.

Worship Resource Guide: Bing, Shirley W. (Worship Chair)"Worship Resource Guide," *SMUMC 1998-1999,* Compiled by the Worship Committee

Figure 25.12:   Jake C. Miller, Ph.D.

Jake C. Miller was born December 28, 1929, in Hobe Sound, Florida.   He holds a B.S. degree from Bethune-Cookman College, and M.A. from the University of IIllinois, and Ph.D. from the University of North Carolina at Chapel Hill.   Miller held professorships at Fisk University and Bethune-Cookman College.   His publications include: *The Black Presence in American Foreign Affairs*, Washington, DC: University Press of America, *The Plight of Haitian Refugees*, New York: Praeger Publishers, Inc.   Miller's articles have appeared in several professional journals.   He is listed in *Contemporary Authors and International Authors and Writers, Who's Who.*

Backintyme
30 Medford Drive
Palm Coast FL 32137-2504
860-468-9631

See our complete list of books at:
http://backintyme.com/publishing.php

Order extra copies of this book at:
http://backintyme.com/ad351.php